Strengthening Families through Fathers:

Developing policy and practice in relation to vulnerable fathers and their families

By Harry Ferguson & Fergus Hogan

About the Authors:

Harry Ferguson is Professor of Social Work at the University of the West of England, Bristol. During the research for this report he was Professor of Social Policy and Social Work at University College Dublin. He is a qualified social worker and holds a PhD from the University of Cambridge. Email: harry.ferguson@uwe.ac.uk

Fergus Hogan is Course Leader in Applied Social Studies, Waterford Institute of Technology. He is a qualified social worker and family therapist. Email: fhogan@wit.ie

First published in 2004

by
The Centre for Social and Family Research
School of Humanities Publications
Waterford Institute of Technology
Waterford

for
The Department of Social and Family Affairs

ISBN 0-9540281-3-9

This research was funded under the Families Research Programme of the Department of Social and Families Affairs. Copies of this report can be obtained by contacting the Family Affairs Unit, Department of Social and Family Affairs, Aras Mhic Dhiarmada, Store Street, Dublin 1. Tel: 01-7034956 Fax: 01-7043594

*Cover Photo: Michael Burke, Hedford, Co. Galway
(with kind permission of John and Ella Byrne).*

Contents

Chapter 1 : Researching Fatherhood and Social Intervention

Chapter 2 : Leaving fathers out: The dynamics of excluding men

Chapter 3 : What vulnerable fathers, mothers and children say about fatherhood, family life and social intervention

Chapter 4 : Developing men who care: Violence, intervention work and the transformation of 'dangerous men' into nurturing fathers

Chapter 5 : Beyond 'protest masculinity': Young vulnerable fathers and social intervention

Chapter 6 : A father-inclusive framework for family policy and practice

Foreword

**Minister of Social and Family Affairs,
Mary Coughlan T.D.**

I welcome this important report 'Strengthening Families Through Fathers' which was completed under this Government's Family Research Programme.

The Families Research Programme was developed to support research projects, which have the ability to inform the future development of social policy and to address the issues that face our society today.

This report emphasises that vulnerable fathers love their children as much as other parents. It also highlights the need for men to be directly included in assessments of their capacities as fathers, unless there is compelling evidence on which to exclude them.

The findings that non-expressive, traditional masculinity keeps men closed off from the skills and emotional capacities required to be good active fathers in the post modern social conditions of today needs to be addressed. The challenge facing us today is to create and foster an inclusive society where effective engagement and positive action by fathers becomes the norm. We must aspire to a society where vulnerable fathers are supported and encouraged to play a more active role in their children's lives for the betterment of all.

This research will inform the effective targeting of resources to where they are needed and raises the awareness of key issues facing society today. This is a key feature of this Government's social policy agenda.

We are very pleased to have assisted the production of this report on a valuable research project initiated by Professor Harry Ferguson and Fergus Hogan into the process that exclude fathers from the bulk of childcare and family support roles.

I would like to thank Professor Harry Ferguson and Fergus Hogan for this excellent piece of research and for their hard work in completing this study. I look forward to the publication of further quality research studies under the Families Research Programme, which is now the responsibility of the Family Support Agency.

Mary Coughlan TD
Minister for Social and Family Affairs

Foreword

Michael O'Kennedy SC,
Chairperson of the Family Support Agency

As chairperson of the Family Support Agency, I am very pleased to welcome "Strengthening Families Through Fathers" which was co-funded by the Family Support Agency and the Department of Social and Family Affairs under the Families Research Programme.

Research is a key responsibility for the Family Support Agency in developing its clearly defined role in the area of family services and policy. The Agency's first Strategic Plan, to be published in May, sets out how the Agency will progressively develop this responsibility during the period 2004 to 2006.

"Strengthening Families Through Fathers" examines what needs to be done to ensure that fathers are included in child care and family support work. The study shows how some fathers are in many respects excluded, often on the basis of their appearance alone. It looks at the role of fathers (young vulnerable fathers, working fathers, separated fathers) in families and talks about the presence and importance of fathers in their children's lives. The research also examines how family members and professionals view fathers, fatherhood and family life.

The importance of families and family life for individuals, communities and society generally is central to the Family Support Agency's strategy over the next three years. In that regard, and particularly in relation to the role of fathers, this excellent research will greatly inform the work of the Agency.

I would like to thank the researchers Professor Harry Ferguson and Fergus Hogan for this excellent piece of research. I look forward to further research studies under the Family Support Agency's Research Programme.

Michael O'Kennedy SC
Chairperson
Family Support Agency

Acknowledgements

Strengthening Families through Fathers was funded under the Families Research Programme of the Department of Social and Family Affairs. The research project has mirrored our own life paths in many ways. When initially commissioned we had both recently stepped into new relationships as stepfathers. During the course of the research we have both changed jobs, moved homes and even, in Harry's case moved to live and work in another country. We have both also witnessed the birth of our own first born children. Through all of this we gratefully acknowledge the support of the Department of Social and Family Affairs. In particular we appreciate the encouragement and family friendly, sustained support we have always received from Heber McMahon.

This report has been supported by a collection of people. We wish to thank our colleagues and friends, in the Department of Social Work and Social Policy, UCD, especially Professor Gabiral Kiely, and in the Department of Applied Arts, WIT, in particular Dr. Michael Howlett. At various times, this work benefited from discussions with Máire O'Reilly, Jonathan Culleton, Geraldine Burke, Alan O'Neill and Colm O'Connor. Patsy Devoy completed the task of transcribing the interviews and did so with great professionalism.

It takes great courage - as well as extra work – for professionals to allow their practice to be explored by researchers and we would like to thank the social workers, family support workers and the social care workers who gave so much to this work. We would like to sincerely thank the staff and managers of the Daughters of Charity and the Good Shepherd Sisters.

Ultimately this report would not have been possible without the fathers, mothers and children, who gave so much of their time, to share so intimately their life stories. These stories of vulnerability and family life are stories of loss, pain and sadness as well as hope, resilience, success and love. Sharing time in their company has taught us both more about family life, fatherhood and the healing power of love.

Finally, we wish to thank our families. We have had to try and fit this research around the pleasures and duties of trying to be good enough fathers and carers for our own children, which has meant that many of the themes of this report have been far from simply academic for us. We owe a huge debt to our partners Claire Mackinnon and Claire Nolan for their love and support. And to our children Katie, Ben, Susie King and Ellen Ferguson; Lorcan Nolan and Caelum Hogan who have taught us so much about fathering and love.

Harry Ferguson
& Fergus Hogan

Executive summary

Many gaps exist in our knowledge of fatherhood in Ireland. These include father's own accounts of what fatherhood means to them, how they 'construct' it and motherhood, and what do Irish men actually do with their children? Moreover, there is a derth of information regarding how social care systems engage with, or respond to, the needs of men as fathers in vulnerable families, what we have called 'vulnerable fathers.'

The objectives of the study and research process

It is now widely accepted that fathers are generally excluded from the bulk of childcare and family support work. The key research question this study addressed, is how can this be reversed, and what needs to be done to ensure that more men are included and become users of child and family services? In this report a 'vulnerable father' is defined as a man who is known to be struggling to be a good enough parent due to having involvement with social services and family support agencies. The report documents a qualitative study based on in-depth interviews with 24 'vulnerable' fathers; 12 mothers; 12 children; and 20 professionals. All of the interviewees came from the same cases as, where possible, we adopted a case-study approach to analyze how men, women and children from the same families and the professionals who worked with them viewed the father, fatherhood, family life and the intervention work they had experienced. The notion of vulnerability we adopted included a wide range of experiences, from men who were vulnerable to being violent to their children and/or partners or were known to have already been, to those who were experiencing a range of problems, including 'marital' breakdown, relationship and communication problems with their children, poverty and the impact of extreme social exclusion, surviving child sexual abuse, addictions, and domestic violence. The sample was accessed through social work departments, family centres, and strategically included only those men who were known to have at least one professional attempt to work with him. Our primary aim was to establish what kinds of inclusive work is going on with fathers, to learn from best practice and to use this as the basis for developing a father-inclusive framework for family policy and practice.

Dangerous masculinities and the powerful dynamics excluding fathers

This study provides evidence, for the first time in Ireland, (and in many respects beyond it), of the ways in which men as (vulnerable) fathers are included (or not) in child protection and family support work. While our primary aim in the study was to move the literature, policy and practice forward by critically analyzing work where fathers were actively included and to build profiles of best practice from that, our data still produced important findings on the dynamics of men's exclusion. We found that the overall orientation of welfare systems to exclude men is so powerful that, even in cases of inclusive practice clear evidence emerged of men's exclusion. All of the men in our sample, despite having been worked with by at least one professional, told powerful stories of being excluded in the past or present. The dynamics of such exclusion took many forms, the most common and powerful of which was a view of men as dangerous, non-nurturing beings. Some men were excluded from being worked with and seen as possibly caring fathers simply on the basis of their appearance and perceived life-styles, such as men who had tattoos, bulked-up physiques, skinheads and who did hard physical violence prone work such a bouncing or 'security'. Yet interviews with the same father's children (and some partners) revealed the complexities of the men's identities in how they were seen as responsible, caring, vulnerable, loving men. This is not to suggest that these men were never a risk to their children and partners. Some were dangerous and known to have been violent and this report documents some of the best work that is going on with such fathers to develop them as safe, nurturing carers. In addition, some men contribute to their exclusion by refusing to seek or accept help. But others, despite being labeled dangerous men, were never known to have actually been violent. They were excluded simply on the basis of stories, appearances, perceptions.

A striking pattern to emerge from our data is the organisational differences in approaches to fathers and families. Statutory social workers are generally much less father-inclusive than voluntary agencies like family centres. The irony is that in many instances including fathers could make social worker's statutory obligations to promote the welfare of children easier to discharge. Yet our findings suggest that social workers generally expect mothers to carry the load, leaving the potential resource fathers have to offer largely untapped. In general, organisational cultures, rather then simply the individual mindset of workers, have the most impact in shaping what form interventions take. This is evident in the striking pattern for the family centres - in our sample at least - to be much more inclusive of fathers than statutory social work. There is something in the very nature of social work and how it is organised and done which is currently antithetical to adopting a more holistic, father-inclusive form of practice. A key factor surrounds the different contexts within which the work goes on. Family centres work within much more 'solid' structures, in that the service is offered on their premises and fathers and families come to them. Social workers, on the other hand, practice mainly in the community and homes of clients, which is a much more fluid process where they have much less control over what they get to see. We found that when family centres have policies to actively include fathers, such as refusing to accept referrals without reference to the father, the men are much more likely to engage. Crucially, engaging fathers is too often not seen as a matter of human rights, unless it is is unlikley that professionals will be motivated to go beyond mothers. Our data shows that many social workers do not actively seek out fathers and try to include them. This becomes a self-fulfilling prophecy as fathers who are around are not regarded as service users and so are rarely engaged with. The net effect is that social workers in general do not 'know' men, have little confidence around them, and often fear having meaningful discussions with them. They also lack skills in discussing fatherhood with men and strategies to divert attention and responsibility for child care away from the mother.

A key finding of this research concerns the need for men to be directly included in assessments of their capacities as fathers, unless there is compelling evidence on which to exclude the man – such as a known history of violence or intimidating behaviour. Education and training of child and family professionals needs to address head on dominant images of masculinity which regard men as non-nurturing beings – and all the more so if they carry markers of being the 'hard-man' on their bodies and demeanours – and which equate caring solely with femininity/motherhood. Our findings show that the most effective father-inclusive practitioners are those who are able to go beyond the one-dimensional imagery of dangerous masculinity to hold a view of men's identities as multi-layered and complex, and containing resources to care for children as well as possible risks, and to develop those caring capacities accordingly.

Changing fathers, changing masculinities

There is nothing from our data to suggest that in general vulnerable fathers love their children any less than any other men. Their struggle is in showing it. Professionals need to begin to include men as fathers from the very start of the process of social intervention and family support. Our data suggests that some fathers need to be invited, challenged and actively brought into this responsibility through social intervention. We refer to this as calling men into responsibility around their children, which we see as a crucial life-changing event and strategy in engaging and changing fathers.

Some very creative and effective work is going on with fathers and their families. This includes regular casework visits from social workers and community based family support workers, intensive family support work in residential type units and day care settings, and less intensive but still regular individual and family sessions at family centres. The types of work being done includes individual sessions with family members, such as direct work with traumatised children; couple work; sessions with entire families together; and parenting courses. A key finding is that changing fathers is not simply about finding ways of equipping them with techniques to manage destructive behaviours, absences and acquiring better parenting 'skills' in some limited technical sense. In every case in our sample where significant change occurred, therapeutic and support work with the men - often in tandem with their partners and children - led fathers to question the basis of their very identities as men and in many respects to reconstruct their masculinity. Gaining the necessary skills to be a good enough parent involves learning about the self - including the impact of how one was parented, acquiring capacities to communicate - active listening, expressing feelings - and engaging in 'emotion work'. A key expression of this changing of masculine identity was in the men's attitudes to help-seeking: the fathers shifted from a view where seeking or accepting help from professionals was seen to compromise their sense of themselves as strong, rational, coping males to one where an acceptance of their vulnerabilities and need for support became integrated into their identities.

Younger vulnerable fathers and social intervention

This study shows that different kinds of intervention work are needed with fathers and families according to their particular difficulties and stage in the life-course. Younger marginalised men who become fathers are perhaps the most at risk, yet invisible category of all. Typically, the position of men in public debates about 'teenage pregnancy' or 'unmarried mothers' is so absent and negative, it is as if the children had no fathers. Moreover, the implications of the (apparent) absence of those fathers from their children's lives is rarely seen as an issue of social concern. Nor is the fact that many younger mothers apparently parent alone, or without the support of an intimate male partner. At its worst, the underlying assumption seems to be that families are better off without such fathers, as they are invariably irresponsible and uninterested.

Typically, young vulnerable fathers are unmarried and therefore have no automatic legal rights as fathers. At its worst they are officially written out of the script of family life due also to the significant pattern of the man's name being omitted from the birth certificate, making it difficult for state agencies to identify the father and mother as a cohabiting couple. In Ireland, most one parent family payments (97 per cent) are paid to mothers, and is done so on condition that the woman may not cohabit. The direct effect of such a condition is to exclude both birth fathers and stepfathers who are in relationships with women on social welfare benefits from (officially) living with their partners and children. This powerful exclusionary dynamic is heavily influenced by the state itself as the social welfare system creates a financial benefit for mothers to claim lone parent family benefit and for fathers names not to be put on the birth certificate, in effect for them not to be seen to officially exist.

Our findings show that, typically, younger fatherhood is unplanned. But this does not mean that it is (always) unwanted. On the contrary, the very marginality of the young man, the absence of other prospects in terms of education and work, can heighten the desire to construct a meaningful life, to see oneself as a worthwhile person and make a tangible contribution through fatherhood. The younger fathers in our sample went to extraordinary lengths to remain involved with their pregnant partners and form loving committed relationships with their babies. They had to, such was the pressure from family and professional agencies to exclude them. If a marginal young man in Ireland today wants to become a committed, involved father with his children, he not only has to deal with the usual joys and challenges involved in such a rite of passage - especially the adjustment to an altogether new form of responsibility - he has to overcome the immensely powerful pressures that exist to exclude him from his child's life. In most cases it is a matter of vulnerable young fathers remaining involved with their children despite, not because of, professional systems.

Our data also shows what can and needs to be done to enable such men to be good enough fathers. The paradox is that while officialdom generally fails to see the presence and importance of these fathers in their children's lives, in reality the men are active, committed carers, and seen and valued by their partners as such. Yet these young men typically also have serious problems, the most significant of which is a 'wildness' and unreliability which makes their consistent support for their children and partner uncertain. A core challenge is to move them beyond acting out what Connell (1995) calls a 'protest masculinity' where their wildness is tamed to the extent that they can adjust to the discipline of domestic routines and remain with their children and partners, in their families (as opposed to prison, for instance). We show that when child and family services do include such fathers, it can only really work best through a model of intensive day or residential family support which work to literally contain the men in their families and fatherhood role, ensuring their involvement in domestic tasks and routines, while helping them overcome some of the adversity in their lives to develop into still better, more reliable, fathers. We strongly recommend the provision of resources by the government to enable the much wider availability of such intensive residential and day family support services.

Intervention work with working fathers

Fifteen of the men in our sample (63%) were working outside of the home. This is no guarantee of relief from poverty and extreme marginality in terms of such things as poor housing, crime and drug ridden neighbourhoods - the fate of some families in our sample. Generally, though, men in paid work were less socially excluded. While men in jobs generally defined themselves as providers, some were struggling to spend more time with their children. Our findings suggest that what being a more active father means to men does not necessarily involve spending less time at work. The men and their partners knew that for the family's survival they had little choice about one of them being a full-time breadwinner, for a mixture of cultural and financial reasons it tended to be the men.

Acknowledging the heroic struggles of poor parents to provide a subsistence living for their children is an essential aspect of best practice with such families. This needs to involve 'being with' the family in their struggle in a manner in which they feel and know their difficulties are understood and being worked with in the interests of social justice, as well as healing. Many of the men who spoke of how family support and therapeutic work had helped them 'reconnect' emotionally with themselves and their families and find ways for them to use the time they did have with their children in qualitative ways which benefited themselves and the entire family. For some men, the emotional component of active child care compensates at least somewhat for the brutalizing effects of hard manual labour and helps to promote men's health in a context of great risk to their physical well-being.

The style of work that was done with the men made a real difference to how they felt. Central to this was an appreciation of a worker's approachability and 'less formal' style in relation to appointments, where workers tried to 'fit' therapy into the already pressurized demands on the couple's life. The notion of 'informality', of speaking 'with' rather than 'to' them, of feeling listened to and not just spoken 'at', was central to what all the men in this study liked about intervention. They distrusted professionals who 'did things by the book', who they perceived as too 'formal' and over-controlling. A sense of 'informality' enabled the men to maintain a sense of control while surrendering to their vulnerability and need for intervention.

Working class men experience tension in trying to show their loving, vulnerable side in a social context which demands toughness and punishes weakness. Joining with men in therapy is about helping to 'equip' them in their journey of un-blocking themselves and discovering their inner resources, and of allowing men to unleash the strength of their own vulnerabilities. The rationale for including fathers in the work is not simply as a support to the mother, or because he has been referred as dangerous and needing to be changed, but because, as one family worker put it, 'we need the father here because he's important. His life is important'. This is preventative family support work at it best in that it enables families at high risk of cracking under the pressure to stay together, so that children are not at risk of entering care and family relationships can thrive on love rather than pain.

Working with separated fathers and families

Ten men in our sample (42%) were separated or divorced from the mothers of the children. Whether separation was experienced in the past or the present, all the men spoke with passion about the exclusion they felt by the family law system, including social services, which they saw as cruelly sexist and anti-man/father. For one sub-sample of men their identity as separated fathers was central to how they defined themselves as service users, and their struggle to be active fathers. For these men, the problem is the family law system, the fact that the courts have been so restrictive in the access given to their children, that the men do not feel allowed to be active fathers. Often their criticisms extended to social services because of their role in deciding custody and access arrangements for children.

Our findings show how, in such scenarios, family workers tended to play a mediating role between family members, the courts and social workers. The striking thing about these men is their anger at the injustices they feel have been done to them. The importance of men feeling listened to and affirmed in themselves and their struggles is a feature of every father we interviewed. It takes on particular significance for those men who feel completely excluded by the system, and whose relationships with their children are under threat because of the judgements of experts. The children in such cases spoke openly of their desire to have relationships with their fathers and some of the best work that went on in such cases was with fathers and their children, to help open up honest communication about the hurts experienced in the family and ways of healing the relationships.

Reconstituted families, love and healing interventions
The men in our sample became fathers in more ways than conceiving their own biological children, nine men (38%) 'stepped' into parenthood by living with a partner who already had children. We included a focus on social intervention work with fathers and 'fractured' or reconstituted families. We were concerned to explore both the risks and resources that stepfathers can be in children's lives. Stepfathers are at particular risk of being ignored by social workers who see themselves as working with women and children. Choosing to work with men as fathers in families requires an assessment of just how involved the man is in the family's life. To establish whether the man is anything more than a casual acquaintance of the mother's, a transient lover, or a man committed or trying to live a life as a father to the children can be a complex endeavor. The interplay of some men's avoidance of family responsibilities, coupled with social workers giving up on what were perceived as disinterested or ambivalent fathers led to some of the men's exclusion. On the other hand, some stepfathers were recognized as being a huge resource for the family to an extent where

children were either not taken into care, or were returned to mothers and their new partners because of the stability and care the latter now offered the family. The intervention work in these cases generally took the form of what we call expressive family support work. It focused primarily on working with the children and fathers to give them the opportunity and means of expressing their experiences and feelings, rather than 'acting out' disruptive and ultimately damaging behaviours.

Developing a father inclusive culture

Our research shows that the more professionals help to keep men distant from their children, the less chance there will be that they will be brought into responsibility. The dilemma for professionals is that vulnerable fathers are all too often initially framed as dangerous and unfit to care, and so calling them into responsibility involves taking a risk. A key area of learning from this study concerns how a dramatic re-framing of the case can go on and men can be moved along a developmental pathway from being a risk to an overall resource to the family. The data also shows that this is not simply a matter of what gets done by single agencies or professionals working alone but emphasizes the centrality of inter-agency perspectives (and tensions) in how father's identities are constructed and reconstructed by professional networks.

At their best, therapeutic and supportive interventions engage in 'emotion work' with men, helping them to recognize the legacy of past events and traumas and how they impact in the present. This involves not only dis-embedding past hurts and destructive patterns, but aspects of traditional masculinity and re-embedding a new, more expressive, aware masculine self. Non-expressive, traditional masculinity, our findings suggest, keeps men closed off from the skills and emotional capacities required to be good enough active fathers in the post-modern social conditions of today. Such encounters with therapeutic and support services have unquestionably helped many of the men in our study develop themselves to a point where they have reached a new integration of the worker/provider and intimate self and become good enough fathers.

Workers who develop the capacity to sit with vulnerable men and call forth their stories set up a positive developmental dynamic within organisations as more positive images of men and stories about effective engagement become part of the culture. The organisational context remains crucial. The proper mix of an open, learning organisation, staffed by well trained, critically reflexive individuals creates not simply a good technical approach to such work, but generates a wisdom and spirit to the work which men and their families feel and respond to. Ultimately, working with fathers in families is not only important for men, but benefits women and children too.

Chapter One

1.1 Background to and rationale for the research

This research report is about vulnerable fathers and their families and the kinds of policies and practices that are needed to enable men to become 'good enough' fathers and promote the safety and welfare of all family members. The report seeks to contribute to the development of family policy by generating original data in relation to families who are struggling to cope, what we call families in need. These are families where the integrity of the family unit is under threat due to relationship problems and parents themselves have recognised their difficulties in being good enough parents and/or partners and have sought professional help, or professionals have initiated intervention to respond to identified problems. Children and families experience adversity in many forms and the aim of this study was to illuminate as broad a possible range of coping difficulties, including child abuse and domestic violence, relationship problems and un-met emotional needs within Irish families. The study is intended to have direct relevance to the development of preventative strategies in relation to child abuse, intimate violence and marital breakdown and seeks to contribute to the development of family policies and intervention practices that are required to respond to them.

1

Researching
Fatherhood and
Social Intervention

The study does this by focusing in particular on fatherhood, and the needs of vulnerable men: what we call 'vulnerable fathers'. This is not to in any way invalidate the needs of women and children in families, but constitutes a strategic focus on men and fatherhood in response to increased recognition of their relative absence from policy and practice agendas (Commission on the Family, *Strengthening Families for Life*, 1998). There has been virtually no empirical research done on fathers in Ireland which explores their actual views and those of the people they live with, this study seeks to contribute to filling at least one aspect of this huge gap in our knowledge, by focusing on families in need through the lens of vulnerable fathers. Changes in family life, gender relations and childhood have meant that men are now expected to be more actively involved as fathers and partners than was the case 30 or even 20 years ago. There is, however, an astonishing lack of social supports for fathers in Ireland and little recognition of the vulnerability of men or their needs (Ferguson, 2001). Vulnerable men in Ireland are in most respects invisible as fathers, rarely even warranting a mention in the plethora of debate about vulnerable families, be it in relation to lone parents, 'unmarried mothers', marital breakdown, balancing work and family responsibilities, and so on. The only real capacity in which some 'vulnerable' fathers are acknowledged in families is as violent, abusive, 'dangerous men'. This is of course of vital importance, but even here the men's status is ambiguous as even violent men tend not to be engaged with by professionals. It is now commonly acknowledged that in families in need fathers are essentially ignored by health and social services providers and that fathers tend to avoid such involvement (Ferguson, 1998; Hogan, 1998; McKeown, Ferguson and Rooney, 1998, chapter 7; Milner, 1996; O'Hagan, 1997). Parenting tends to be regarded as synonymous with mothering, and it is with women and children that professional relationships are formed. This means that fathers are not engaged with about their role or the parenting - what we call 'fatherwork' - they do, or would like to do, with their children. Any problems fathers may have are not dealt with, thus contributing to the risk of trauma and family breakdown. In addition, the potential resources of help and support that fathers may already offer, or have to offer their children and partners in families in need is largely

Any problems fathers may have are not dealt with, thus contributing to the risk of trauma and family breakdown

untapped. In effect, the starting point for this research was the fact that little attempt is made to engage fathers or develop men as carers.

Research has begun to become available to support clinical/anecdotal evidence that this neglect of fathers applies to all services. The recent major evaluation of the Springboard family support initiative in Ireland has shown the extent to which this exclusion of fathers applies even to those services which have been strategically established to work with entire families at risk and in need.

> one element of the family system that is routinely ignored by most family services is fathers. Despite the best efforts of Springboard to engage fathers, we have seen that the vast majority of Springboard time, even in two parent households, is devoted to mothers and children, although we have no reason to believe that fathers, both resident and non-resident, are any less in need of support services or are any less affected by the well-being of the family system. The pattern by which family services tend to ignore fathers reflects a tendency among service providers to treat parenting as synonymous with mothering. It is doubtful if such selectivity between parents – which no doubt is reinforced by a process of self-selection by some fathers themselves – is consistent with a family support service in the fullest sense of the word family. Accordingly, we recommend that services to families - which should not be treated as synonymous with services to households - should give careful consideration to all elements of the family system and offer supports in a holistic and inclusive manner.
>
> (McKeown et al, 2001, pp 120-1, emphasis in original)

This crystallises perfectly the stage at which research, knowledge and practice are at in relation to vulnerable fathers: there is evidence of significantly increased awareness of men's exclusion from intervention work with families, but with little idea or attention given to how this can be changed or what 'father-inclusive' work might look like. There exists an almost total absence of engagement strategies in relation to fathers. Against this background, the core research question explored in this study was how can more (vulnerable) fathers be effectively engaged with by social care services more of the time? The core method we adopted to answer this question was to seek out cases where it was known that at least one professional or service had made real efforts to engage fathers. We have attempted to learn from fathers who have been service users by eliciting their views on the services they received, how, or if, they were helped, and what constitutes best practice. Similarly, we sought to learn from a sample of mothers and children from the same families as the fathers their views on services, practice and what constitutes effective interventions. We explored similar issues with the professionals who worked with the same fathers and families to enable us to build up a picture of what effective engagement of fathers involves. This enabled us to identify a range of issues, variables and processes which influence the degree to which agencies and individual workers are 'father-inclusive' and arrive at a composite picture of what constitutes best practice with fathers and families.

... how can more (vulnerable) fathers be effectively engaged with by social care services more of the time?

The deficits in what we know about such fathers goes well beyond ignorance of how services can effectively engage them. Little is known about vulnerable father's definition of themselves as fathers, their experiences of being fathered/parented, their feelings about their children and what they actually do as fathers and partners, their views on professional intervention and what they feel they need in order to be good enough fathers. This research report generates original data on these questions. It also produces original data on the roles and experiences of mothers and children in families in need, how they view their own lives and the men/fathers in their families and how they evaluate the professional work done with them. The report also generates original data on how professionals construct interventions with children and families, their views on gender relations, the role of fathers and the kinds of work they actually do - or don't do - with men and families. Mothers and children were included in this way in the research design because it is now broadly accepted by family researchers that the meanings of what constituted 'a family' and how roles and relationships are lived out need to be explored with the range of actors who are involved with one another in defining and living out those roles and relationships.

1.2 Aims of the Research

The aims of the study can be summarised on four levels:

- To document the needs and perspectives on fatherhood and family life of vulnerable fathers and their partners and children.

- To examine the factors and processes which lead to the exclusion of fathers from child and family services.

- To examine the factors and processes which lead to the inclusion of fathers in child and family services and to identify good professional practice with fathers and their partners and children.

- To identify best practice and develop a framework for policy and professional intervention with vulnerable fathers and their families.

1.3 Theoretical orientation: a developmental perspective on vulnerable fathers

The research was framed in a context where theoretical perspectives on fatherhood are beginning to change from 'deficit' approaches, which focus simply on issues of fairness in child care and domestic work, and what fathers don't do in families. Research focused around the issue of 'domestic democracy' has shown that in general mothers carry the primary responsibility for child care and housework, although the balance of who does what in particular households is multi-layered. Fatherhood and family researchers have begun to develop 'generative' approaches which seek to identify and build on the positives that men bring to their father role (Hawkins and Dollahite, 1997; McKeown, Ferguson and Rooney, 1998, chapter 4). This is not to deny the parenting deficits that some men may experience, but to focus strategically on developing men's capacities to care and nurture. A focus on 'generativity' - the capacity to care for the next generation - is at the core of a new developmental perspective on fatherhood (Hawkins, et al, 1995) which seeks to enhance men's capacities and practices of 'generative fathering' (Hawkins and Dollahite, 1997). This research study adopts a theoretical perspective which is based on the need to develop family policy in ways which advance (vulnerable) men's abilities to practice generative fathering. Thus we are seeking to move public debates and family policy beyond the position articulated in much of the existing policy and practice material, where a 'deficit' model views men in a negative manner, for example, by focusing on men who have been violent or abusive and more generally the attitudinal 'un's' where fathers are depicted as uninterested, uninvolved and unable to parent. This study is significantly different in that it does not simply focus on categories of abusive men but generates data in relation to the needs and potentials of a wider range of men and fathers. A working definition of families in need draws from instances where (a) professionals have expressed concerns about parent(s) abilities to function as 'good enough parents', or (b) where parent(s) have expressed their own sense of inability to cope with their parenting and relationship tasks. Thus we defined a 'vulnerable father' as a man who is known (by social service agencies) to be struggling to be a 'good enough' parent.

... we defined a 'vulnerable father' as a man who is known (by social service agencies) to be struggling to be a 'good enough' parent.

1.4 Methodology

The research questions and aims of the study required methodologies which could generate extensive qualitative data about the experiences of families in need, vulnerable fathering and professional intervention. In seeking to develop an actual model for intervention with families in need it was necessary to have detailed first-person narratives of father's experiences, as well as other family member's and professional's experiences. The core sample in the study consists of 24 vulnerable fathers/families in need. Families were only included where there were fathers available - whether resident or non-resident - and where at least one professional or service were known to have made attempts to work with the father. While there is no doubt there is something to be learned from examples of how fathers are completely excluded by the system, the primary aim of this study was to learn from instances where men were worked with. That said, a key finding of the research was that exclusion and inclusion are not mutually exclusive experiences, as all of the men in our sample, despite attempts having been made to work with them, related stories of being excluded in the past and present.

Semi-structured interviews were conducted with 24 fathers, 10 mothers, 11 children and 19 professionals. Separate semi-structured interview schedules were constructed for the fathers and mothers, children and professionals. All the interviews, which lasted on average between two and three hours, were tape-recorded and transcribed. The lower number of mothers is explained by three factors: (1) the unavailability of the women in some cases due to not being service users; (2) women who were service users but did not wish to take part in the study; (3) the decision by us as researchers not to interview every mother, but a representative sample so as to leave time and resources for us to prioritise the inclusion of as many fathers as possible. Similar explanations exist for the lower number of children. Some children were of course simply too young, and rather than seeking to interview all the children and young people who were old enough to invite to be included we sought to include a sub-sample who represented experiences of the kinds of family problems and intervention approaches in the sample. Thus given the primary focus of the research, the sample of service users is strategically biased in favour of gaining the perspectives of vulnerable fathers, but with significant input from mothers and children also.

We aimed to interview at least one professional involved with each father/case and because some professionals worked with more than one case, the sample of 19 professionals covers almost every case[1]. Eight of the professionals were statutory social workers employed in Health Board community care teams, while 11 were family centre workers. A further crucial dimension to the research method was a case-study approach

---

1   We missed professionals in a few cases because they pulled out of arranged interviews at the last minute due to pressures of work or sickness, or because they had left the job.

where we sought to interview more than one key actor in the same case, and ideally all the key actors involved. Thus in some of the case studies documented in the report we interviewed as many as five or six people involved, including fathers, mothers, children, social workers and family support workers. This approach has the advantage of giving voice to as many stakeholders in cases as possible and also allowing us as researchers to develop a variety of perspectives on the same events and processes. This practice of 'triangulation' of data strengthens the validity of qualitative research as we are not required to base interpretations and recommendations solely on the accounts of single respondents in cases. We were able then to develop our findings on best father-inclusive practice out of a rounded picture of what fathers, mothers, children and professionals said about how intervention 'worked'.

. . . the sample was strategically designed to include families where it was known that at least one professional or agency had made strategic efforts to work with the father in the family

We sought to include families who fell along a continuum of social exclusion/inclusion: from the most disadvantaged who have contact with such agencies as homeless services and statutory social work services, to 'middle-range' struggling families who are involved with family centres, youth projects etc, to the least disadvantaged families who use services like family centres and counselling services. The intention was to explore the experiences of vulnerable fathers and families across the spectrum of social exclusion/inclusion.

The families/fathers were accessed through a number of sources: family centres, residential centres which cater for homeless mothers and children, and the caseloads of health and social services workers. The agencies mediated for us by passing on a letter of invitation to take part to all prospective respondents. Permission to interview children was given by the parent(s) already engaged in the study. To further enhance the validity of the data, we avoided taking all the cases from just one organisation and place. We included organisations which work with children and families and cases drawn from two geographical research sites: One in an urban area in the East of the country, the other in the South. The identities and exact location of all the participants and services have been disguised in order to protect the anonymity of the families and individual professionals involved. As already emphasised, the sample was strategically designed to include families where it was known that at least one professional or agency had made strategic efforts to work with the father in the family. We were not interested in including cases where no efforts were made to work with the fathers as we reasoned that nothing could be learned about how to work with fathers and their families from cases where fathers were excluded, other than about the dynamics of exclusion and its effects on women and children, as well as men. This biased the sample towards intervention work which at the very least had a positive outcome, in the minimal sense that someone tried to include the father. The selection of family centres, for instance, was influenced by the fact that managers advised us that the centres involved were known to have made efforts to work with fathers. Similarly, we asked social workers to tell us about the cases where they had tried to work with fathers as well as other family members. We have no way of quantifying how much of the work we profile in this report is going on nationally. Yet even in the context of examining 'father-inclusive' practice we still found a great deal of evidence of exclusion of fathers in the very same cases. If fathers are being excluded by some parts of the system in the midst of some of the best work that is going on, then we shudder to think what is happening in the worst case scenarios, which we suspect are extensive. What we can also say with some confidence is that some very committed work is going on with fathers in families in a context where professionals are struggling to find ways to engage men and models to work effectively with them. Thus our sample contains cases where intervention work was effective, where men, and women have been helped to become better, and perhaps even 'good enough' fathers and mothers; and also where intervention work failed to adequately engage fathers. The perspectives of fathers, mothers and professionals were analysed to produce data which deepens our understandings of the needs of vulnerable fathers, mothers and children and for the development of models of intervention with families in need, especially around generative fathering.

The sample size is clearly small, as is necessary in such qualitative studies to generate the kinds of detailed narratives from fathers and others that are needed. The qualitative method we used involved an awareness that the scale of findings that can be produced from a large survey, for instance, would not produce the kinds of in-depth data we required to explore our research questions. We made a conscious decision to sacrifice such quantitative data in favour of the extraordinary level of detail from the narratives of a relatively small number of respondents that is necessary to fully explore the meanings of interventions and identities such as father, mother, child, and 'helper'. In fact, the qualitative case-study method we employed is extremely time-consuming in terms of producing and reading transcripts of interviews and the analysis it demands.

1.5 Problems the families experienced in the sample cases

In finding appropriate fathers and families we were indebted to and dependent on the agencies who gave us access to their service users. There are however gaps in the profile of vulnerable fathers, especially concerning the absence of traveller and other ethnic minority men and their families from the sample. The sample cases ranged along a continuum of seriousness in terms of levels of concern for the safety and welfare of children and adults and the risks of children coming into care. Cases placed along this continuum, starting at the most extreme end, involved:

- ■ 'high risk' child protection situations where legal action had already been taken and children were on supervision orders - due to non-accidental injury (NAI) and emotional abuse.

- ■ children were at grave risk of coming into care - due to suspected neglect, homelessness, domestic violence, alcohol and/or drug misuse.

- ■ histories of domestic violence, NAI and extreme 'marital' problems - leaving fathers in need of help in caring for their children, some of whom had significant mental health problems.

- ■ younger parents without a stable relationship and settled living accommodation whose child care was considered 'neglectful' and borderline abusive.

- extreme difficulties arising for children and their parents from poverty, social exclusion, and trying to survive in dangerous communities inhabited by drug dealers and suspected sex offenders.

- fathers surviving histories of childhood sexual abuse and growing up in families where there was extreme domestic violence.

- relationship problems between parents, children and adolescents, including concerns about drug and alcohol misuse.

- fathers who have primary responsibility for childcare, lone fathers who live with their children full-time and non-resident fathers who's children live with them for some of the time.

- couples work, negotiating relationships roles and responsibilities, mediating separations, and supporting access arrangements.

This list does not of course exhaust all the kinds of problems child and family professionals work with. It was beyond the scope of the study to cover everything! We are satisfied, however, that the sample has enabled us to profile the broad range of problems and types of work that are going on and that need to be developed in work with vulnerable fathers and families.

1.6 The structure of the report

The report is divided into 6 Chapters:

An introductory Chapter (Chapter 1) is followed by two Chapters (2 and 3) that provide overviews of our findings. Chapter two explores the dynamics of how fathers are excluded form child and family work, while Chapter three discusses what fathers, mothers and children said about fatherhood, family life and aspects of the intervention work that was done with them.

Chapters four and five present detailed case- studies which seek to illuminate both general and specific issues in working with vulnerable fathers and their families. This detailed analysis of our findings through the use of case study material focuses on issues of dangerousness and risk, (in chapter 4), and how men adjudged to be a danger to their children and parents were worked with in ways which helped to develop them into nurturing fathers. Chapter five examines the issues arising from intervention work with younger vulnerable fathers. While Chapter six concludes the study by drawing together the various strands of our findings and presenting a framework for 'father- inclusive' policy and practice.

Chapter Two

The exclusion of men from social work and social care work intervention is now quite widely noted in the literature (see, for instance, Buckley, 1998; Scourfield, 2000). Yet the actual dynamics of such exclusion, the belief systems, organisational processes and practices which lead fathers to be excluded have not been clearly demonstrated. By 'exclusion' we are referring to the ways in which men are ignored, avoided, or actively kept out of child and family work by professionals and how men absent themselves, or are kept out by other family members. Our primary aim in this study is to move literature and practice forward, by critically analysing work where men were actively included, and from that, build profiles of best practice. Despite this, our data produced important findings on the dynamics of men's exclusion. The overall orientation of welfare systems was found to exclude men so powerfully that even in cases of inclusive practice clear evidence emerged of men's exclusion. It is important then for us to document this, and promote learning about the dynamics of exclusion as a means to raise awareness of and reverse such patterns.

2.1 When excluding men appears legitimate

The exclusion of men from intervention work is multi-layered, with many forms and conse-quences. It is crucial to point out that it is not

2

Leaving fathers out: The dynamics of excluding men

always an undesirable thing and can be a legitimate strategy, and good practice. There is a key distinction between avoiding the man per se in awkwardly trying to pretend (or wish) that he wasn't there, and excluding him from work with the family because it is viewed as better for them if he is not included in their lives. In the latter scenario, the man is consciously and openly excluded from 'family work' and rationales given for this, as it is viewed as being in the best interests of the children, and partner. A social worker in our study articulated this point as follows:

...I've one case where the parents are separated and the dad has a huge, huge, desperate effect on his kids in terms of like huge domestic violence and is quite violent towards his kids. I wouldn't try and engage him, I wouldn't, you know. I know he'd be down in the house every day and might stay over a couple of nights, but I wouldn't try and engage him because I'd be you know trying to encourage the mother to you know bar him completely from the house. And every time I would encounter him he would, it wouldn't be of any use to you know the kids at all. So I wouldn't.

... He would talk to me, yeah. More often than not he'd be very annoyed or if I see him there's obviously some very serious incident that's happened that he wants to give out about you know. The only times I would have really ever seen him was when he's been violent .... So I wouldn't actually you know try and work with him at all.

(female statutory social worker)

The social worker here consciously took up a position as an ally of the mother to assist her in protecting the children and ultimately trying to exclude the violent partner:

the family presents as a single parent family and I know that the mother would be very reluctant for him to know everything that's going on. So I wouldn't, I wouldn't diverge from that you know. With this particular family I think they need to be encouraged to work for themselves rather than having his influence around the whole time, and being scared of him.

2.2 When excluding men is problematic

The key issue, however, concerns the basis on which the decision to exclude the man is reached, if indeed it can be said that a conscious decision has been made at all. Our findings show a powerful pattern of men being actively excluded on what often appeared to be for good and solid grounds at the time, but what in reality was the flimsiest of evidence. In general, we found that to speak of exclusion and inclusion as distinct phenomena is simplistic. In reality, they often coexist, while one agency works with the man, others may simultaneously be excluding him, or have excluded him in the past. Even within the service provided by the same agency a man may have been excluded in the past and now be included, or vice versa.

Three factors inter-relate in making some practitioners more father-inclusive or exclusive than others:

- Occupational cultures and institutional norms

- Personal biography and constructions of gender and parenting

- Professional training

A striking pattern to emerge from our data is the organisational differences in approaches to fathers and families. Statutory social workers are generally much less father-inclusive than voluntary agencies like family centres. The latter in our sample had taken more time, as organisations, to reflect on gender roles and accommodate the recent social changes in parenting roles, and the transformation of intimacy in families. The father-exclusivity of statutory social workers reflects how health boards are more reactive, and less institutionally thought-out in their approach. This, our data suggests, is intrinsically connected to the ways such agencies go about their work and the contexts in which they inter-face with fathers and families. It reflects the messier context in which statutory social workers have to work, where the presence of men in households is often unclear, sometimes deliberately so, as the family conceal the man's residence in the home because it helps them to gain more welfare benefits. When there is more than one father to the children social workers are often unclear about where, or how, to focus. The ambivalence of mothers about including their partners (or ex-partners) is also a significant factor. Some mothers appear to have little conception of themselves other than as the primary parent and want social workers to themselves, as it were; others want the men excluded because they feel they are useless, irrelevant or because they fear them.

The irony is that including fathers could make social worker's statutory obligations to promote the welfare of children easier to discharge

The kind of clarification work that is needed to establish the role of fathers in families, and try to engage them takes energy, insight, critical awareness, focus/commitment and skill. Our findings suggest that these qualities are often absent. Crucially, engaging fathers has to be seen as worthwhile. Otherwise, social workers will not be motivated to attempt it, and go beyond mothers. Dominant constructions of masculinity permeate everything, and service user men generally are seen by social workers as dangerous, useless, and 'behind the times' in relation to societal changes in gender roles and parenting. While we found traces of this thinking in family centres, especially the idea that vulnerable families have not changed with the times, family workers generally took a much more holistic view of men, masculinity and fatherhood. These professionals and organisations had a capacity to see the multiple sides there are to men, going beyond superficial images of dangerousness and fecklessness, which meant that they engaged much more fully with fathers and in creative ways, which developed them as carers.

The irony is that including fathers could make social worker's statutory obligations to promote the welfare of children easier to discharge. Our findings suggest that social workers generally expect mothers to carry the load, leaving the potential resource that fathers have to offer largely untapped. Even if it is not seen as legitimate to work with the father as a potential resource because the man is a problem or threat - neither are they worked with as dangerous or feckless men. Thus father-exclusivity is not good child or woman protection practice either. Further, men who have been abused by their partners are not worked with as victims/survivors.

While professional orientations are crucial to how cases are constructed, the responsibility for, and outcomes of, engaging men are not professional's alone. The response and orientation of service user men themselves and what they bring to the encounter is crucial if effective engagement is to occur. This was typified by fathers who took responsibility for their own fears and resistances to receiving 'help' and getting involved with professionals:

> *Well it mightn't be even an attitude that they have...it might be an attitude that you have you know. As I say, when I first went looking for help I had this attitude that I don't really want to be here, you know, I don't really want to tell this person this. You know, so you're on your guard straight away and I don't know whether social workers are trained in dealing with that but most people that go and talk to these people are, they're on their guard going in there you know, they have this shield around them that they're not going to let down.*

Practice is best understood as a co-construction between all of the key stakeholders involved. This father is quite right: professional's levels of engagement skills are crucial to the effectiveness of working with men, and our findings suggest these need to improve significantly. Equally, the personal and professional blocks, the 'shields' that keep professionals away from men need to explored and addressed.

Family centres have no statutory requirement to promote the welfare of children and work with families, but are generally more active in assessing and using the parenting resources available in families by including fathers. The entry of clients/users into such services is generally 'cleaner' than for social work in that the service has more control over who it engages with and on what terms. This is most effective where referral criteria are laid down by the agency which are 'father-inclusive' and is easier to manage in that professionals are frequently (and in some services the only) referral agents. Yet, where social workers who refer cases have not done the initial clarification and engagement work with mothers and fathers, and not included the latter in referrals to family centres, family workers are left to resolve these difficulties and try to include men.

These are not absolutes, however. Some social workers are more father-inclusive than others, and not all family centre workers have the same passion for including men. It is here that the influence of personal biography and constructions of gender and parenting come into play, along with the impact of professional training. Also of relevance is the frequency and quality of supervision, and the views of managers and supervisors. All of these issues are expanded upon in the chapters that follow.

2.3 The forms of exclusion and dynamics of excluding men

The exclusion of men from child and family work takes numerous forms and dynamics. 'Forms' refers to the types of practices which exclude the man, 'dynamics' to the processes and rationales through which exclusion is practised.

The most thorough form that exclusion takes is institutional exclusion, two types of which were apparent in our data:

1. Fathers in prison. Although not available to parent when incarcerated, the general pattern is for them not to be worked with as *fathers* despite the knowledge that they would be released into the community and be returning to their families. Once back in their families, we found evidence that little was done to include them or help them to find a place back in the family and develop their relationships with their children and partner and their parenting skills. The exclusive relationship with the mother established when the man was absent continued. Again, these were not absolutes in our data as some family centre workers included incarcerated men in 'family work' by visiting them in prison, accompanying the woman and doing couple work with them and dealing with child care issues.

2. Men excluded from active fatherhood by the family courts and social services through restricted access to their children. This either creates problems that require social intervention (by family centres, counselling services) or compounds existing problems in the family. Eleven of the fathers in our sample (46%) had exclusionary experiences of this kind at some stage in their family history. For some, the entire reason for their involvement with child and family services, was the impact on the children and father of marital breakdown, and family law difficulties.

Five patterns of rationalisations emerged from our data through which the dynamics of exclusion were manifested:

- Few men around, it's mainly single-parent mothers

- Working class men slow to change

- Men as difficult, dangerous

- Enough to do working with mothers

- There need to be obvious benefits to including men

2.3.1 Few men around, it's mainly single-parent mothers

A powerful justification by statutory social workers for not working with fathers is that there are "so few men around". This creates a rationale for the work as really being about single-parent mothers.

> "the amount of fathers on my caseload isn't huge, considering the amount of families I do have."

> ... it's a lot of single mothers, single mothers who would have maybe two or three children with two or three different fathers with no contact. You know, people who've moved around a lot.

Yet our interviews showed that many social workers do not actively go after the fathers and try to include them. This becomes self-fulfilling prophecy, as the fathers who are 'around' are not regarded as service users and rarely engaged with. The net effect is that social workers in general do not 'know' men, have little confidence around them, and often fear having meaningful discussions with them. They also lack skills in discussing fatherhood with men and strategies to divert attention and responsibility for child care away from mothers. Fathers spoke eloquently of how they recognised such processes, which occurred even in situations where fathers themselves made efforts to engage, after social workers had initiated contact:

It just got crazy. Oh social workers were involved yes. The social work system is so clogged up, they've got so much on their plate for the limited resources they have that we never really see them and I think they need an awful lot more help themselves! You know in general. Because ... I've gone up to their centres and I've seen the girls (sic) just don't have half the people or the time to put into half the people that need it you know. So the little bit of help that I got from them, which wasn't a lot, I got more help from [the family centre] a lot more help from here.

The same father was very critical of the lack of considered response, even at the time when he had battered his wife and the social workers intervened.

That was basically it. There was no kind of counselling, there was no kind of chats, nothing, no follow-ups, no nothing! ... And god knows, anything can be going on in people's houses, you know, unless the people chase them themselves. I had to, I had to go and sit in with me kids, eventually, just sit there and wait to be seen.

2.3.2 Working class men slow to change

All the professionals we interviewed believed there to have been very significant social changes in gender and parenting roles in recent years, with a shift toward the sharing of household tasks and active involvement by fathers in the care of their children. The dynamics of where the typically marginalised families who use services fit, in terms of traditional and post-traditional families was very well captured by one family worker:

"The families that come from here are very, very traditional. Even the food they eat is traditional. You know they haven't tried Chinese they haven't tried Indian. There's the bacon and cabbage and spuds and stews and you know it's like taking families out of the, you know, 30 years ago. You know this particular part of society in general has changed but this group of families hasn't actually moved with the rest of it you know. I think society has changed I think because both parents are working you'd have to. You know what I mean. In other areas of life and stuff like

I think women and girls are brought up different now as well you know. They're not brought up to sit at home they're brought up to have careers and things like that you know, there's aspirations around your daughters as well as your sons now, umm, to have a life outside the home but that's not saying that everybody wants a life outside the home or anything like that but you know. I don't think, girls aren't taken out of school early any more and boys left there. You know that type of thing doesn't happen any more, in most of society. Unfortunately for these people they don't go to school they don't, they don't have the same traditions as people who may be middle class or who'd have better lives you know they've less chances and things like that you know."

(Family centre manager)

A statutory social worker exemplifies how our professional respondents saw social change as manifested in their own lives and families:

Yeah! I think it's [fatherhood] changed completely. There's a photo over there of two of my brothers just looking up and they're both changing their babies nappies you know and you know my mother was just there, my god, times have changed!

... [my father] was completely you know old-fashioned. Went to work, came home, you know, more potatoes [wife's name], you know that type. You know, a great father but completely, you know, my mother would go away, she'd go away for a week's holiday or something and she'd have the dinners ready for him to heat up. ... but he's gotten much better now because we're all grown up and we just go WHAT!, you know, so now he realises that ... But it's funny, I've four brothers and to have my four brothers parented that way by their father and they're so different to that.

Both these quotes acknowledge changes which sociologists refer to as a 'transformation of intimacy' and as a shift from traditional to post-traditional fatherhood and parenting (Beck and Beck-Gernshiem, 1995; Giddens, 1992). Gender roles are no longer fixed in the traditional mode where men were the breadwinners, and respectable masculinity was defined in terms of the 'good provider' role. Women's identities were cast solely in terms of caring and meeting the physical and emotional needs of families. Due to the increased participation of mothers in the workforce, men are now the sole breadwinner in only half of all families with dependent children in Ireland (McKeown et al, 1998). This means that while some families still conform to the traditional model, increasingly the norm is for family life and 'intimacy' to be negotiated as men and women decide who will work, what hours, who will do the washing-up, cooking, child care and so on. It is against this background that some social scientists argue the family is becoming more 'democratic' in form, as roles and relationships have to become negotiated, with children as well as between parents (Giddens, 1998).

Yet while all the professionals in our study regarded these changes as significant - in both their own and people's lives in general - they are not seen as being equally distributed among the social classes, a view which was apparent among both family workers and social workers:

> *[we need to] bring home to them that like it's their responsibility. I think sometimes fathers don't realize that they have as much of a role as mothers do. And that they need to realize that. And that you know this is the, I was going to say the '90s, but 2000's you know. What I mean is that it's quite normal for a father to parent on his own even you know it doesn't have to be and that you just need practice because I think it's something that men don't actually you know take on board very, certainly the men I've worked with would still have quite an old-fashioned view that the mother, it's the mother's job you know. So just to kind of be very clear that they have as much responsibility as the mother to parent the child.*
>
> (Female statutory social worker)

This social worker is getting at what we refer in this report as *"calling men into responsibility"* around their children, as a crucial life-changing event, and strategy, in engaging and changing fathers. Our data suggests she is quite right that some fathers need to be invited, challenged and actively brought into this responsibility through social intervention. We are less convinced, however - at least on the basis of the evidence from this study - that working class and marginalised fathers do have value systems which are that different to the societal norm, and their middle-class counterparts. Our scepticism arises from the finding that so few male clients are actively engaged with by social workers about their views on parenting. Social workers views are largely based on their observations and what mothers tell them. While this is never of course irrelevant, it should be obvious (though it is not) that the inclusion of men's voices is essential to constructing a complete picture of the meanings and practices of fatherhood. Once the father's voice is included, as it is in this study, a much more complex picture emerges of men's views on, and practices of, fatherhood. Given that the majority of our respondents were from working class backgrounds, our findings show that these men are aware of social change, and living out the changing nature of parenting and gender roles. Indeed, our findings suggest that a core aim of social intervention (even though it was rarely expressed by respondents in quite this way) was to push them along this developmental path to be good enough 'post-traditional' fathers in democratic families. Interestingly, professional's belief that fatherhood has in general changed for the better, to a more active model, was no guarantee that those same professionals would try and promote such progressive models of fatherhood in their work. We found workers who, despite strong beliefs that more active fathering was a change for the better, did little or nothing to enable the men on their caseloads to progress along such a developmental path. Here we argue that not only occupational cultures, but professional's biographies, have a particular impact in terms of attitudes and the influence of how they were parented themselves, on their approach to service users as parents. In effect, implicit and explicit contrasts are made between social professionals, families in general, and client families who remain the traditional, dangerous 'Other' in welfare work. This links child and family work profoundly to issues of social class and difference. Scourfield (2003), on the basis of his research into gender and child protection, speculates that, in a cultural context where men 'as a problem' has gained increasing purchase in the media, and where men who sexually abuse are seen as universally deviant - even within the humanist discourses of social work - giving men in general a bad name. Pejorative discourses of masculinity have some value for staff who work in child protection in making social worker men seem all right, seem safe. 'The dangerousness of rough working-class men is implicitly contrasted with the respectability of other men (Hearn, 1990; Edwards, 1998), and male social workers themselves are among the respectable men' (Scourfield, 2003, p. 105). Yet our findings suggest that this goes beyond just constructions of dangerous and 'normal' men, to entire belief systems about the supposedly traditional practices of mothers as well as fathers in families on the margins.

2.3.3 Men as difficult, dangerous

For many social workers men are seen as immensely difficult to engage, as impatient and unwilling to be challenged or brought into responsibility for their children; as more trouble than they are worth. These two social workers exemplify this perspective:

"[if] men get intimidated at all they just withdraw and they just step out of it. Whereas women I find are a bit better."

there wouldn't be that many fathers involved. You're really working with single parent families, the fathers might be around but they're, I've a couple at the moment, but on the whole I think men more so than women feel way more threatened by somebody like me advising them on different you know parenting issues. Or the fact that we're coming down to the house you know obviously you know investigating and assessing their capabilities and I suppose my experience is that men find that an awful lot more threatening than the women. And that would be just my client list you know. And that whilst the men are around that they don't want to necessarily engage with the social worker. They're frequently more likely to become verbally aggressive: "You can speak to me through my lawyer, I'm not going to see you without my lawyer being present". And another frequent thing I've come across with men is if they do anything for their kids, you know, as I said before, they feel as if they've made a sacrifice: and "oh, aren't I great that I've come to help the kids out", you know.

We found that in a minority of cases the fathers were indeed reluctant to accept social work intervention. But, for the most part, the men we interviewed were effectively engaged with by at least one professional or service. Thus it is not just the perceived 'difficult' nature of the men involved that it at issue, but the kind of services fathers are offered and the engagement strategies that make a crucial difference to the effectiveness, or otherwise, of efforts at engagement.

2.3.4 Enough to do working with mothers

The problem of excessive demands on time permeates everything social workers say about their work. Statutory child and family work is invariably pressurized and crisis-driven. In this context working with the mother seems like both the best use of time, and, possible route to reducing professional stress levels.

> *Working with the kids and the mother is time-consuming enough, never mind trying to engage with him. Because he's not going to engage at any real level, you know.*

2.3.5 There needs to be obvious benefits to involving fathers

There is a degree of selectivity in including men that is unthinkable in relation to women. Social workers have to feel that there are "obvious benefits" to including the father before they can be sure he is worth the effort.

> *"I'm bringing this guy [father] in as much as I possibly can who hasn't got all the baggage maybe that [other 'dangerous' male client] has, and whether that's right or wrong, I suppose it's more obvious that he's a benefit."*

Thus, not all men are ignored and excluded by social workers but one implication is that it has to be earned in a way that (good) motherhood, as a condition for being engaged in intervention work, would never be. The double-bind for fathers is that they have to prove themselves worthy of professional attention before social workers engage with them to give them that chance to prove themselves. The requirement to 'prove themselves' becomes all the greater given the routine negative assumptions about marginalised fathers that social workers bring into their work and the other processes that impact on the construction of men in child and family work. Little wonder then that so few men do get the chance to prove themselves.

2.4 The power of 'embodied' masculinity as an exclusionary dynamic

Of all these exclusionary dynamics, notions of the dangerousness of men were particularly significant. This rarely stood alone, but was cast within representations of 'embodied masculinity' (Connell, 1995; Scourfield, 2000), where certain dominant ideas are expressed about the violence and material power of men. Our data suggests that such exclusion took place through two further processes.

2.4.1 Physicality: The man is judged negatively on the basis of his presentation, appearance, his tattoos, 'hard man' persona, lifestyle - such as doing hard physical work or aggressive, violence-prone work, like bouncing, or 'security'. As one father recognises:

> "Being from the [part] of the city I have tattoos, a lot of people would actually judge us by the way you look, cops especially and social workers, they take you on the way you look. People would say to me that I look rough and ready. There's people judging you, probably that's what's wrong with me like, there's nothing wrong with tattoos, I see nothing wrong with them. It's just that where I was brought up I got tattoos and whatever I don't know but I'm just caring too..."

Overcoming this kind of prejudice and classism is essential to including marginalised men and often involves challenging other professionals and family members representations of the man. As one statutory social worker observed of her work with this father:

> "Dad wasn't in the picture. Mum had given a very bad account of dad and said that he was very abusive to her, that he had been violent toward her and really he wouldn't be any fit parent really for the girls. I spoke to a social worker in the hospital who was very much against dad. Like, he looks, you know, he has the

tattoos, the shaved head you know and I think she just felt, you know, on presentation alone that he just was like, you know, we won't even go there."

2.4.2 Mythical story telling: A powerful exclusionary dynamic surrounds the stories that float around the system about the man, usually about his dangerousness, but also fecklessness, and the various attitudinal 'uns' - uncaring, unreliable, unable, unwilling. This is typified by a father who - the social worker explains - had been represented by past social workers, the social work team leader and his partner, as being;

"incredibly emotionally abusive to her, having a loaded shotgun by the bed and bullets, leaving bullets on her pillow and, you know, hitting her. But that wasn't the main thing, it was more emotional stuff. He just allegedly had no interest in the kids. She did absolutely everything and, you know, he kept kind of the purse strings and all that kind of stuff."

This all had a powerful impact on the social worker who avoided meeting the man, the only contact was through the occasional telephone call:

"I was quite frightened of him because I believed the stories. It was a given that they were true. So I phoned the odd time but he really unnerved me, because, you know, his manner. But if you have all these stories behind that manner then you think there's something kind of weird. Whereas he's just got sort of a gentle soft-spoken manner, maybe now. I'm not convinced, you know, I'm not, I just don't know. He had like, everyone, the whole family had everyone stumped you know, all the professionals just stumped you know".

It turned out that once efforts were made to engage constructively with the man, he was a good enough parent to be given full responsibility for child care. This mythical story-telling then goes hand-in hand with the silencing of men, the failure to give them voice. The man's identity is constructed by professionals, sometimes in collaboration with family members, without any direct reference to the man himself. The stories are mythical in the sense that they are never grounded in what the man has to say about himself or a careful assessment of his risks and capacities as a parent or intimate partner.

2.5 Excluding fathers: An exemplary case

'Frank' exemplifies the binds vulnerable men can find themselves in with social professionals. In most respects his treatment by professionals exemplifies all the exclusionary processes identified in this chapter, in one case, and will therefore be used to draw the strands of this chapter together. The father was in prison for 8 years for a sexual offence perpetrated on a woman. The mother, here called Susan - 'a chronic alcoholic' (social worker) - and children were in and out of a homeless hostel, on one occasion for an 18 month period. According to the social worker "things have been rocky with her" and the work attempts to get her to "stabilize". The children have been in and out of care, usually on a short-term basis, the last time being 4 months earlier for a week in care on an emergency care order. Frank was out of prison and he and his partner went drinking. The mother was on the streets drinking "with her old buddies" and "became extremely violent towards the guards". Now the professionals are "monitoring" the family. Entering care is extremely stressful for the children, "being away from mum" being the main source of their stress.

In relation to social work contact with father in prison, there was "absolutely none". Some contact was made with a probation officer, however. A few months before his release the social worker began to talk with the mother about her feelings and plans. She had remained in contact with Frank throughout his sentence, despite having a child to another man. She proved "hard to pin down" however, because of the "double-edged sword" of wanting Frank back in the family as a support, but with the fear of drawing child protection concerns onto them because of his history. For the social worker, "we didn't know [Frank] from the man in the moon either at that time. We didn't know what he'd want, we were going on what [Susan] was saying."

For the social worker "child protection stuff was in my head with the impact of [Frank] coming back. I suppose [Susan] had portrayed [Frank] to us [as] the wronged hero kind of thing you know." The social worker accepts that "he served his sentence, you know, he did his time and he has a right to be out of prison and to be back with his family." But she is still concerned about the child protection implications:

I suppose the first thing that came into my head was OK, three very small children in the family with a mum that isn't always able to protect them and the oldest child sexually abused in care by an uncle. Um, extremely, extremely vulnerable.

Yet when she met Frank she felt somewhat reassured.

I think it's like everything, I think when you concoct a picture in your head about someone you haven't even met it's like the fantasy is always worse than the reality. Um, after meeting [Frank] I suppose it changed a lot of my own thinking as well in that he's not the brute or whatever you think a person who's in this situation is going to be. You know, I suppose it challenges your own values of what, you know, a criminal is ... Because he's actually quite a quiet man. I mean he's very in your face and he's a big guy and, you know, there's potential for him to do anything, but at the same time he comes across as very non-threatening.

The father was actually out of prison and at home for 2 weeks before the social worker even met him. She had however met Susan and monitored Frank's impact through her and how "she'd come into the office and even just seeing her and how relaxed she was since he came out portrayed a picture that you know maybe here, ... I feel he changed her."

The focus of the work was on supporting the mother: "subtly getting stuff in there around parenting because [Susan] was very closed off to anything to do with us teaching her about parenting or anyone teaching her about parenting. And as far as she was concerned parenting was not an issue, she was able to do it." The children were not easy to manage, especially when they returned home from care. A child care worker was going in three days a week and doing most of the work, while the social worker rarely called (perhaps three or four times in the two months since the children returned from care) and acted as a case manager. Little wonder then that for the social worker the mother "sees me as a person who calls when things are bad."

The social worker took a gentle approach as she didn't want to "overwhelm" Frank at first:

I suppose I'd a feeling that he was going to be seeing us too as in there whether he liked it or not and I just didn't want to be going in there putting all the stuff on him either, that he was going to feel like I have no [say] here, I have no control over my own children or whatever. So I suppose I just went out to enlighten him more than anything else as to what is there, what's been going on since he's been away, what's there now and that we are involved and remaining involved and for him to think about what he wants ... around the children.

However, the father's response was not encouraging for the social worker:

He just sat there, he didn't say much, he didn't really engage with me. I was doing most of the talking to the point where I said OK I'll leave this with you, you know, you get back to me and we can talk further. And that was it. I went a couple more times I think before the kids actually came into care.

The children stayed in care for just a week, but the 'father-exclusive' pattern was established. When the social worker called to the house the father would leave the living room and:

walk into the kitchen. He tended to let [Susan] talk to me and ... the child care worker would be the same. He tended to let whatever was going on just carry on and he'd kind of steer outside it. Whether he felt uncomfortable in it or whether he felt he didn't have a right to be in it I don't know.

The problem was the social worker never asked him why he was the way he was. The social work practice never went beyond this superficial level of "enlightenment". The social worker takes some responsibility for not being more proactive in engaging the father, but still sees him as the source of resistance. She did make some efforts, "looking to them for what are their ideas, what do they want, to keep trying to draw him in at that stage. But he was still quite guarded. I felt he was, kept himself on the fringe, let [Susan] kind of deal with us."

The social worker was asked in the research interview to reflect on her approach to the man's behaviour and apparent resistance:

I always had the feeling that he wasn't comfortable with us coming up, most men aren't anyway.

Interviewer: *Did you ask him?*

Social worker: *No I didn't. I didn't actually ask him, thinking back, yeah. I suppose I didn't really. I tended to inform him of the nicer things like, talk to him about the nicer things. You know, kids doing whatever, preschool and like that that might draw him in and he mightn't be threatened by us or whatever, I suppose.*

There is an powerful assumption here that openness about more serious issues is antithetical to engaging resistant service users. Yet, as the fathers told us, it is precisely workers' failure to take them seriously and include them in meaningful dialogue about their lives which compounded any fears or suspicions the men had about involvement. The social worker is unambiguous in relation to the more serious child care issues. She ignored the father and focused on the mother as the primary client: "definitely it'd be her. T'would be [Susan]."

I have talked to the two of them together but it's more really, to be honest, if he's there I talk to him. If he's not there, he's not there and whatever I'm going up for is dealt with, with [Susan]. ... but there's practical constraints on me. If he's not there, I'm not going to be calling up again to see him.

While the social worker said she had to change her "framework" of thinking about the family once the father returned home from prison, in reality she continued to see herself as the mother's social worker. One implication is that child protection is synonymous with motherhood and enabling mothers to parent safely and well enough; or at least does not involve engaging in a meaningful way with fathers about their children. Frank was not even engaged with about the fact that his daughter was sexually abused while in care, although Susan told the social worker that Frank had very strong, angry views about it.

Yet, on balance, Frank is regarded as a positive influence:

Despite everything I do think he's a stablising factor for her [Susan]. I know that sounds totally contradicting [sic] what I just said, but I do think he has made a huge influence. I think he's taken a lot of the practical pressures off [Susan], taking the kids to school, getting the dinner ready, the whole thing, getting them up to bed and I think that's been a stress for [Susan], the ordinary stuff has been a stress for her. ... So I think he's been a stabilizing factor there alright. But I suppose considering what's happened, that it's a case of we know now that if they are going drinking, that there's issues around violence. Violence wasn't an issue but it is now. Somebody has to be aware considering what has happened.

The irony is that while the positive contribution that the father is making to his partner and children is acknowledged, he is never told this, or affirmed in any way. Nothing whatsoever is done to develop him or ensure that he does those things as often as possible.

In his research interview, Frank emphasised how he knew that, as a convicted sex offender, his identity has been spoiled and he is seen as inherently dangerous. The fact that he completed a sex offenders treatment programme in prison was ignored by social workers. On his release from prison, one professional in the community advised him to 'keep his head down' and try not to be seen. Yet, having initially tried, and failed, to prevent him from living in the home again on his release from prison, social workers basically ignored him. He disliked this because he resents not being included in on-going work and decisions concerning his children, yet he does not feel safe challenging social workers to include him, because he fears that drawing attention to himself will possibly lead to the removal of the children, or him, from the family. On balance, it feels safer for him to keep his head down and try to seem *"not to be there"*. The costs for him are that nothing changes. Or at least he is not seen to change, which he believes he has, with the support of a family centre. He remains excluded from the social work, yet speaks very highly of the family support work done with him now, and over the years, by the mother and child unit.

Concerted work by family workers revealed that prison had completely institutionalised him - he didn't know how to cook or clean even when he wanted to. He was terrified of open spaces, feared being judged by people in the community and became almost agoraphobic. He was able to leave the house if accompanied, but could not leave the children to school as this would mean returning home alone. In prison he lived in the solitude of a single cell and returned home to find the noise and activity - especially at night - of a youngish family intolerable. Simply nothing had been done by prison staff or the criminal justice system to prepare this man to live again in the community, which is precisely what the family workers had to put great efforts into doing. It is the capacity of very vulnerable fathers to sustain their commitment that is often in doubt, not the nature of that commitment as such. When their partners are vulnerable mothers and unable to offer stability either, there is a very high risk of severe family problems and breakdown and the situation for the children is dangerous. By the time we interviewed Frank, however, he had been out of prison for 5 months and was beginning to settle into an active fatherhood role. He was leaving the children to and from school, cooking, cleaning and much else.

This shows how the ambivalence of service users in presenting themselves as users - entitled to a service - often arises out of a context where they, or their partner, has a troubled history where there is a real risk of the children being taken into care. A younger father, Sean Whelan (see also chapter 5), struggled to have a relationship with his child while his partner was in a special unit, trying to prove to social workers that she was a 'fit mother'. Her first child had already been taken into care, and Sean's presence was not viewed as a positive thing by social workers which led him to maintain a low profile, despite his great commitment to his child and partner. Thus he too never challenged the social worker - or indeed his partner - as they disappeared into the kitchen to talk exclusively. A further powerful reason for not wanting to be 'seen' by state officials was that because it ensured the family had more money to live on the mother claimed lone-parent allowance and officially the couple were not co-habiting.

If a father has a questionable past or present in terms of, for instance, violence, this aspect tends to overwhelm all other professional perceptions of him, including, and perhaps especially, his capacity to parent. The most effective father-inclusive practitioners are able to accommodate a complex notion of masculinity as multi-layered. They recognize that there are many sides to men and masculinity and that they need to go beyond representations of dangerous (and feckless) masculinity - what we call 'toxic masculinities' - to give the other (nurturing) parts of him a chance. This does not mean avoiding the dangerous or irresponsible elements of what is understood about the man, but needs to involve directly confronting and, where necessary, working with these toxic aspects in tandem with a focus on the man's capacities to actively care for his children well enough.

If a father has a questionable past or present in terms of, for instance, violence, this aspect tends to overwhelm all other professional perceptions of him . . .

Our data suggests that we need to move away from simple dichotomies of 'bad man-good woman'. However resistant and difficult men often are to engage, some/many workers regarded women generally as just as, and sometimes more, aggressive and threatening.   Significantly, stories about 'dangerous women' simply do not circulate around the system in the same way as they do about men. The very notion of a 'dangerous woman' is not openly articulated in this way, despite there being women who are experienced in this manner by professionals. This appears to relate to the mythical dimensions of constructions of gender which are embodied in violent imagery about men and caring stereotypes of women.   Professionals feel they have to work with women if children are to remain in the family, which means attempting to access their caring side, even if it appears distant and submerged. They are disposed to looking for signs of generativity and nurture in women, while in men they struggle to get beyond the often mythical signs of danger. There is a material basis to this in that professionals know some men to be capable of very serious violence, especially against women.

Underpinning all these exclusionary influences is the powerful dominant belief that men don't care about or for children, that they can't care, won't care. This exclusion is underwritten by law, as well as by cultural practices. Many of the men in our sample were unmarried fathers who have no automatic legal rights as fathers and have to apply for guardianship. The logic of the social welfare system also discriminates against men as women exclude them to claim single-parent benefit. Men collude in this as, with his single-person state benefit, the combined income of the couple surpasses what they could get as a cohabiting or married household. There is also the significant pattern of the man's name being omitted from the birth certificate, to make it difficult for state agencies to identify the father and them as a cohabiting couple. The net effect is that marginalised men are officially written out of the script of family life. Layer upon layer of powerlessness become piled upon one another, to produce an outcome where the man accepts what he's got, living a shadow existence outside of the gaze of officialdom. While this survival strategy works on one level, as the family unit is together, it fails in other ways as it leaves the man without any supports - he does not really exist - as far as the outside world is concerned. This endangers the very integrity of the family that it is intended to preserve. This is rarely seen as a loss, as men in general tend not to be viewed as nurturing beings or seen as having any capacities to develop as carers. The gendered corollary of this is that women do care, should care, and through intervention will be made/helped to care.

The exclusionary dynamics we have set out here can appear singularly or in combination. The more there are, the greater the struggle to include the man. When all are present the exclusionary dynamic is immensely powerful. Yet our data suggests that even in those circumstances it is still possible for workers to reframe their definition of the case, and construction of the man, in purposeful ways, to enable father-inclusive practice, and we will show in this report how this can be made to happen.

Chapter Three

Many gaps exist in our knowledge of fatherhood in Ireland. These include father's own accounts of what fatherhood actually means to them, how they 'construct' it and motherhood, and what Irish men actually do with their children? Vulnerable fathers are particularly intriguing in this regard perhaps because of their marginal status. As we have already pointed out, our sample reflects a continuum of experiences and backgrounds, from the poorest, most socially excluded fathers and families, to a middle-range group, to the least excluded. In general, the narratives of the men in our sample reflect the fact that fatherhood has been undergoing significant changes in recent years. With just one exception, the men not only demonstrated a capacity to reflect on their identities as men and fathers, but showed how such reflection was a constituent part of their identities as fathers and partners. This shows the degree to which gender has explicitly become a key organising variable in everyday life (Connell, 1995). Gender identities were (implicitly) on the agenda of their relationships, and a major focus of social intervention.

Most of the men remained rooted to at least some degree, in a breadwinner and provider model of fatherhood. They were either happy to be at work, and away from the demands of family life, struggling to break free of it and spend more

3

What vulnerable fathers, mothers and children say about fatherhood, family life and social intervention

active quality time with their children, or had already done so either through unemployment, marital separation, or a choice to be the primary parent. These men's identities as fathers should not be seen in a static way. The men were invariably involved in a process of development. Their own fathers were generally described as being in the traditional provider mode. Some still identified with their fathers, feeling loved, but most men felt that how their fathers had primarily showed their care was through going out to work. The men's fathers - as well as the types of problems which led to social intervention - were invariably used as a standard against which the men were seeking to become something different. This chapter considers how the men viewed themselves as fathers and the developmental process of fathering they were engaged in, and their general perception of social intervention work that was (or was not) done with them. It also includes the views of the sample of mothers and children on similar issues.

3.1 Vulnerable men's development as men and as fathers

We strategically designed the interviews with men in such a way as to be able to track how they had developed, or not, as fathers. We were interested in exploring the men's 'developmental pathways', that is their experiences, levels of involvement as fathers and self-definition from the time of conception and birth of their first child, both as an interesting finding about fatherhood in its own right, and as a means to understanding the impact of social intervention, and where it fitted in terms of how the men had developed - or not - as fathers. This, not surprisingly, proved easier to track for the older fathers who had more years of experience to reflect upon, but was also possible for the younger fathers.

Men's assessments of themselves as fathers could be strikingly honest:

> I was shite, pure unadulterated. I made excuses about work and everything else, but it wasn't, I wasn't there and I should have been and that's what has changed. ... They know now in no uncertain terms if they're in trouble or there's a problem that I am there. And we'll try and sort it out. You know so that's the difference. At the time, yeah, sure, I'd never make father of the year by any stretch of the imagination! Things have changed, things have changed.

Such comments reveal the particular context out of which this data on fathers and families is being produced, that 'betwixt and between' state, where the men reflect on their past identity and performance as a father and compare and contrast it with how they see themselves today. The father just quoted is typical in that going back many years he had had significant problems in his marriage, with gambling addiction and his children had been in temporary care. Past experiences of social intervention were very negative for him as he did not feel understood or supported by social workers. The most recent phase of intervention he saw as having a major influence in enabling him to become, as he saw it, a much better father. Central to this was his recognition of the impact on him of childhood sexual abuse and getting significant therapeutic help to enable him to heal. He was now in a new relationship and forging meaningful relationships with his new step-children, as well as healing his relationships with his birth children. Intervention work by a family centre worker was enabling him to learn better how to recognise his feelings and pattern of trying to control and impose himself in relationships and enabling him to communicate with his partner and children in an open, equal way. It is important, then, to do justice to the 'then' and 'now' aspects of men's stories and the role of a variety of influences on the development of their lives.

There is nothing in our data to suggest that, in general, vulnerable fathers love their children any less than any other men. Their struggle is in showing and applying it. Taken as a group, the vulnerable fathers we spoke to were, at various times in the past and present irresponsible, wild, violent, absent, drunk, gamblers and in other ways reckless with money, abusing drugs, careless, controlling. But they were also loving, affectionate, generous, compassionate, hard-working, caring, sacrificial, concerned, wise and supportive. Most desperately wanted to be good-enough fathers to their children and many saw social intervention as helping them to achieve that. Nor, our data suggests, do vulnerable fathers perform any less direct care for their children than the amounts that research shows men in general who are not the subjects of social intervention perform (Lewis and Warin, 2001; Kearney, et al., 2000). In some crucial respects, vulnerable fathers are the same as all fathers; they are every man. Yet it is crucial also to acknowledge that vulnerable fathers, by virtue of a level or type of vulnerability which has necessitated social intervention in their lives, do have specific needs and represent particular dangers, to their children, partners and themselves. Our sample of vulnerable fathers were at various times in the past and present sad, depressed, suicidal, lonely, self-harming, violently angry, fearful of responsibility, physically sick from abusing drugs and alcohol, exhausted and physically harmed from over-work, traumatised by childhood abuse or from present violence, and suffering from the injuries of poverty and the corrosive impact of social exclusion.

We do need to be careful in making such generalisations. Many of the fathers we interviewed told us of the great joy and wonder they experienced on becoming fathers. Others revealed real ambivalence, that their children were neither planned, nor wanted and the best they could expect was to grow into the relationship and fatherhood role. Yet we would expect to find the same variations in the general population of fathers.

3.2 Becoming fathers: Birth experiences

All of fathers in our sample attended the birth of at least one of their children. Those who didn't make it to all of the births mostly blamed outside pressures and poor communication as the reason they didn't get there on time. The degree to which expectations that fathers should attend births have changed, is exemplified by one man who still feels guilty because he missed the birth of his first child 10 years earlier due to being at a work *"night out"* in a restaurant. Despite he and his colleagues constant telephone contact with the hospital, he still didn't get there in time, admitting that having several drinks didn't help. One younger father was convinced that his, by then ex-partner, had been pressured by her mother into not telling him she was in labour, which he truly regretted. Another younger father had to overcome extraordinary barriers, especially lack of money, to travel 70 miles to the hospital where his partner had their child. He deeply regretted missing the actual birth through no fault of his own, but was there for his partner and baby soon after.

Without exception the men who were present found the birth experience profound:

> *"I actually was a little bit late getting in for the birth, she had actually just had the child but they hadn't cut the cord, not yet. It was brilliant, life. But to see it is something else, it's absolutely fantastic! I would recommend it to anybody."*
>
> [50 year old father]

They celebrated in different ways, the most common being a trip to the pub. One young father spent a whole day there and 300 pounds *"wetting the head"* of his baby daughter with his mates, and anyone else lucky enough to have walked into the bar that day. The importance of being present at the birth is that it can help start men on a developmental path of active fatherhood, based on an immediate bond with the child and a strengthening of the relationship with their partner:

> *Brilliant! Brilliant! Can't explain it like, I remember the time, the day, I remember everything, I can remember the whole day. D'you know, and the two of them. And there's a kind of a connection then with myself and [partner] you know, a stronger connection because I seen the child being born...*
>
> [Raymond Jones]

The second (and less common) pattern to emerge was of stories dominated by a struggle to accept parental responsibility and even outright denial of it. Some men simply never wanted to be fathers. One father exemplified this in a narrative of an adult life which was organised around trying to prove his (traditional) masculinity. While he does recall attending all of his three children's births, because their lifestyles (heavy drinking and drug use) and the marriage (violent and unstable) were so chaotic from the outset, he has little memory of being involved with the children in the early years and can remember nothing of his 15 year old daughter as a child at all. His celebrations on first becoming a father at 19 (unplanned - "nothing in my marriage was planned") had less to do with the joy of bringing his child into the world than with having proved his manhood:

> *"I thought it was great! I was going to be a dad, and it worked: I was able to make somebody pregnant! It was not a kind of a fatherhood thing, it was, I don't know. No I never looked at it like that at all."*

Such men clearly have a very significant journey to travel in developing themselves as fathers and our data shows that, while some men remain stuck or constantly struggling, social intervention contains real creative possibilities in enabling this to happen.

3.3 Stepping into fatherhood

The men in our sample became fathers in more ways than conceiving their own biological children. Nine men in our sample (38%) 'stepped' into parenthood by living with a partner who already had children. Indeed, one of the men had never had a child in any way, and was about to take up the care of his partner's sister who was to be accommodated with them from care and was included to amplify the lived experience and needs of such men. Some men felt that their bonding with their 'step-children' was as meaningful as if they were their own children. Dermot Casey found that his encounter with his new partner's 4 year old son Justin was the beginning of a healing relationship for him. Justin had witnessed his father abuse his mother and Dermot himself was a survivor of a very violent father:

> "[Justin] he's me son, he's me stepson right? The trouble he had with his father it's just, that's why I related so well to him, when I met him because he, he reminded me of me, you know what I mean? I actually, I was the same way like because I knew how he was feeling because I used to feel that way."

This identification was the source of healing for not only the child, but the step-father. Becoming a stepfather was something that Dermot spoke of as having been quite 'natural' for him to do. It was as he put it quite simple, he was in love with his partner and he knew that he could not have her without the children. Dermot believed that Eve's story of living with a physically violent partner reminded him of his own mother's life and was one of the reasons they seemed to get on together so quickly, sharing an understanding of the impact of living with domestic violence.

The love and commitment in step-relationships grew from the man falling in love with the mother, and accepting her children as part of being with her. For some vulnerable mothers, this can even be a pathway to an altogether more secure life for her and her children, where they can actually be together. Joanne and her four children aged from 16 to 4 years (by three previous partners) had no stable home and the children were in care. Then she met Seamus, a 29 year old manual worker, with whose help they got a home together. According to him he took to step-fatherhood with relative ease:

"Well I felt it from the first day you see kids. Joanne already told me what to expect being a father you know. And she said things aren't going to be totally easy you know but I like having kids around the house, roaring and shouting don't bother me at all. I bonded with them an awful lot you know. I think after about a couple of weeks like yeah the first couple of weeks they got to know me and I felt the bond. I mean it took them a while to say daddy alright you know. But they're all, they're all pretty good now. We're a real family unit now."

Some men are a huge resource to vulnerable mothers, without whom the women would struggle to keep their family together. This father willingly attended every meeting he was asked to by social services to determine the placement (at home) of the children, and left no one in any doubt about his commitment to his new family. It is not the biological connection between men and children which determines the quality of the relationships, but the openness to giving and receiving love, and the amount of work the parent is prepared to put into making that relationship work. The degree of commitment to the relationships and active fatherhood seems to be the key.

"I'm not their father their actual father like you know. But I'm their real father you know, looking after them. Which I think I'm doing, to do everything right for them and keep looking after them and when they're going wrong, they must be told what to do right. Stuff like that you know, that makes a real father. ... I kiss and hug them all. And show them as often as I can. I'd tell them I love them when they're going to bed now and that, and I'd tell them I love them in the morning even if they are in a bit of a rush."

(Seamus)

3.4 Constructions of gender and what vulnerable fathers do with their children

The majority of men saw the mother as the primary parent. This did not always reflect their preference but revealed the reality, as the men saw it, of how children tend to gravitate to the mother.

"I suppose fatherhood means parenthood it's being the second role of parenthood. Um you know I suppose motherhood is the primary role. That the way I see it or well yeah it's jointly you know it's...it's....I suppose it would be, it should be equal like."

(Philip)

"Because I'd say they're fond of her like, they're fond of, they're fond of the mother because like the mother's there. Like it comes from the mother, and I think that inside in the hospital with her and so often the mother rears them and the father does half but I reckon the mother comes first. It's the same thing if you go to court and you're fighting about the kids the mother will get them quicker than the father. Because it's the mother first, the mother would get them before the father first. In a family like the mother comes first because they came from her, gave birth. Like you, you've only one mother you could have a thousand fathers. You know what I mean?"

(Jason)

"Being a father is being there for me children. That's the way I look at it like just be there for me children they need me. I can be there for them... The mother is the one always in the house like you know with the kids like you know. Like even when I'm there now or Martha's there the kids are all Martha. You know. But like if Martha is gone out to the shops or anything like that like the small fella there now like he'd be up in her arms he'd be, I'd be sitting down he won't be near me then she'd be gone to work and it'd be daddy this daddy that. Everything'd be daddy then like you know. But eh like when Martha's there she's number one with the kids that way. She'd be number one like mammy this, mammy that like you know. I feel alright I know you know the way we were all kind of you know, it was always mammy this or mammy that..."

(Frank Valentine)

"Obviously I can't give them the motherly love, I give them the fatherly love. The difference is the mother you know had them in her belly for 8 months, 9 months sorry. And um it's just it's just a maternal instinct for children to have the little edge over the father for their mother and that's natural. I think every animal has that and I mean they're animals...at the end of the day."

(Paul Smith)

Others regarded women's greater involvement in child care as a social thing and a product of the greater opportunities there are for women to develop relationships with children while the men work to provide. Some believed that both parents should be equally important, even if the man is out working, which is part of his importance to the family unit.

"I mean it's pretty simple, any dick can be a daddy, you know what I mean, but it takes more to be a father. I mean you've got to be there."

(Paul Smith)

It might be assumed that the more marginal and *'problematic'* the family/man the less interest he has in child care. Indeed, as shown in chapter one and throughout this report, our findings show that many social workers hold to such a view. The most marginal men in our study were in fact more likely to be actively engaged in domestic work and child care than the others. This is partly to do with their greater availability at home, due to unemployment. But it also reflects two other things: the men's values in terms of how they wish to be as parents; and the impact of intervention work on the men which had helped them to get closer to and do more direct caring of their children.

The single most socially excluded category of person in Irish society is prisoners, some 99% of whom are men. Prisoners score highly on every indicator of social exclusion, including poverty, educational disadvantage, poor housing or homelessness, long-term unemployment, and estrangement from family (O'Mahony, 1998). To our knowledge, at least 5 of our sample had experienced prison. While only seeing your children once a month during a lengthy incarceration is bad enough, the big problems for such fathers begin when they get out, as the experience of Frank Valentine who served an eight year prison sentence for sexual offences,is highlighted in Chapter Two. Yet with the help of the mother and child unit, Frank made considerable progress in applying himself to active fatherhood:

"Well I don't know if my mates know that I love my children or not you know but I know that I do. I, I give out to them if they've done something wrong like I, you know, I do that like. But eh I, I just every night when they to go to bed like and stuff and I give them a kiss and I tell them I love them and all that like. The same thing in the mornings when they run out to school like you know I drop them down to school every morning and before they go into school I give them a kiss and all that like and do things with them and stuff like you know. I bring them swimming down to the swimming pool all the time you know. What keeps them happy and I'm happy. [Wife] will go but she won't get in the water! You know they're good kids in their own way like you know."

(Frank Valentine)

If anything, we found the most marginal men talking down what they did in the home and with their children, such as one man who literally slept in the ditch outside a homeless woman and child unit so that he could be near his family.

Interviewer: What other things would you have done with the children then when they were young?

Father: When they were young? When they were down here [in the mother and child unit] first thing when they come home, when they come home I'd do is make sure they get their homework done. And then they can go out playing then come in and have their dinner and the whole lot. And I'd be gone then I goes away then about we'll say about half nine. I'll go away about half nine tonight. Sometimes then I could be there in the morning I could call in if I've no job on, I'd just call in and make sure the kids had gone to school and the whole lot...

Interviewer: When you were living together with Sandra and you had all the children like who would have done most of the housework?

Father: Well the two of us did the same. She could be doing the front room now and I could be inside washing the ware. And after that then we'd go upstairs and start making the beds together. And then work down the hall and...The kitchen would be last...the kitchen. The front room, the front room would be first, I'd be doing the ware then and the pots and the whole lot. Then we'd go upstairs and make the beds and start sweeping the rooms down the stairs and wash the clothes upstairs and down the stairs and down the hall. So in other words when you come down the stairs the whole room would be done... the hall...and then you've the kitchen, and bathroom. Well...I'm just, you do your share in everything...give a hand and all that.

Raymond Jones, a 23 year old father of two children under three, began taking drugs and drink at the age of ten, has been in prison and lived a wild and dangerous life, including stealing, driving and burning fast cars. Yet he talks passionately about his commitment to his children and has always - by his own and his partner's account - provided good care for them at times when his relationship with their mother is stable, including getting up in the night to feed and see to them:

Well it depended, you know. I didn't mind, I wanted to get up you know. If Ann was getting up I'd say stay in bed, I'll get up, that's the way I was. Because I didn't care as long as I'd the baby in me arms, then I was happy, d'you know what I mean? I don't know, I suppose it's all different for everyone like you know.

In relation to whether this father does a fair share of the work with the children, he felt: "I do me best like, you know. I do me best for them. You can't do any more." There used to be arguments about who did what:

but no not any more, because I just say sit down and she just has a rest or she'd tell me sit down like.
What used you argue over?
Oh, stupid things, you know what I mean, always over stupid things. Me missing all

day or something like.

You missing all day...?!

When present, marginal young fathers are capable of contributing a great deal to the household. It is their propensity to go "missing all day" and barely even see the significance of it that creates real problems (see also chapter 5). Research has shown that what men do at home is typically a contested issue, with men generally rating their involvement in domestic chores and child care as greater than how their partner's rate it. We were keen to interview a sample of partners to establish their views of family life and constructions of fatherhood and gender roles. We have no way of objectively establishing the 'truth' of the claims made by respondents. What we can do is analyse men's, women's, as well as children's accounts for indicators of differences and consistencies in what they said and possible reasons for them.

Raymond's partner, Ann, represented him as a good, indeed a "brilliant" father, really valuing his contribution. But she also emphasised his unreliability. She never knew when/if she could really trust him. She herself was a vulnerable mother, a young woman with a history of drug misuse who was now receiving full-time family support in a homeless mother and child unit. The unit had also begun to work strategically with Raymond to develop them as parents together and as a family unit. Engaging men and keeping them involved in therapeutic and support work - what we call 'holding' men - is one of the biggest challenges professionals face in this work. Our findings suggest that the forms of work achieved by such residential or intensive day care type facilities is often necessary if the intensity of intervention work and structure that is required to develop such vulnerable parents is to be provided.

3.5 Working with separated fathers and families

Almost by definition intervention into the lives of vulnerable families involves dealing with relationship breakdown or the risk of it. Ten men in our sample (42%) were separated or divorced from the mothers of the children. The experiences of separated men in our sample took a number of forms. Some became the lone parent responsible for the day-to-day care of the children while non-resident mothers had different degrees of access to the children. These men used social services and family centres to gain therapeutic support to help them develop as parents. Other men were non-resident fathers typically in custody and access disputes over their children, the trauma of the contested separation and adversarial family law system was the main reason why their children and themselves needed therapeutic support. Whether separation was experienced in the past or the present, all the men spoke with passion about the exclusion they felt by the family law system, including social services, which they saw as cruelly sexist and anti-man/father. For one sub-sample of men, their identity as separated fathers was central to how they defined themselves as service users and their struggle to be active fathers. For these men, their problem is the family law system, the fact that the courts have been so restrictive in the access given to their children that the men do not feel allowed to be meaningful active (good enough) fathers. Often their criticisms extended to social services because of their role in influencing decisions about custody and access arrangements for children.

Our findings show how, in such scenarios, family centre workers tended to play a mediating role, picking up the pieces from the strained relationship between the family members, the courts and social workers. The striking thing about these men is their anger at the injustices they feel have been done to them. This is so manifest and 'in your face' that the real danger is that all professionals see is the angry, aggressive man and not the loving, caring father. Our experience in the research interviews attested to this. The importance of men feeling listened to, and affirmed in themselves and in their struggles, is a feature of every father we interviewed. But it takes on particular significance for those men who feel completely excluded by the system and whose relationships with their children are under threat because of the judgements of experts.

Our interviews in these cases of contested separations highlighted the deeply conflictual he said/she said nature of accounting the 'truth'. The narratives make clear that there is invariably a history of marital discord yet what seems beyond doubt is that in these cases it is the men who lose (custody of) their children and often their home. As a consequence many of the separated fathers have nowhere to bring the children, to have reasonable quality contact since they moved out of the family home. The problem often is not just the amount of access per se, but where to have it, and in a place that does not cost a lot of money, be it the stereotypical McDonalds or some other commercial outlet:

> I've got limited access. I can see, listen to this, I can only see my children, the two youngest ones, 2 hours once a week on school days, 4 hours once a week on weekends. I must give my wife a week's notice, right! Now that sounds lovely doesn't it? You know what, d'you know how long 2 hours lasts? It'll take me a half an hour to get the kids back and a half-hour to take them, that's 1-hour. So basically I've got an hour with 2 children.

Many of these fathers articulated their feeling that 'nobody wants to listen to me', and with such a depth of anger this may not be surprising, in that the anger may frighten, alienate and push people away. A number of these same fathers had become quite politicized through joining father's rights organizations, where they learned that they are not alone and that 'the system is stacked against fathers'. While other men in our sample made generalisations, they tended not to position themselves as representing all men in their situation. However joining a father's rights organisation allowed men to meet other men like them and gain an even greater sense of injustice and develop a campaigning sensibility. In the research interviews these men repeatedly quoted other men's cases so as to prove the veracity of their own case. Fathers in this situation clearly have a powerful sense of not being believed. However, having become politicised in this manner brings with it a type of narrative closure. While these men tend to want to speak for all such fathers and want to change the system to prevent other men from experiencing what they have, it is more of a struggle with such men to get a personal narrative, to get beyond the man's anger to an intimate sense of him as a man and father.

Overall, however, fathers who end up in contact with family support and social services primarily due to a 'marital' breakdown and ceasing to live with their children have particular needs which services need to become better at responding to. Given that so many have been extensively excluded from their children's lives this anger has a righteous basis to it and these men's 'political narratives' (of rights/exclusion/marginalisation/injustice) need to be understood within a political framework using a model of 'healing and reconciliation work! This in some way needs to recognize the injustice of the situation (on all sides) and move the process forward by creating space for new /alternative futures and ways of being actively involved fathers.

Yet we felt satisfied that some family support services managed to achieve this. Some men recognised a key role in father inclusive social intervention, what we are calling 'expressive work'; which involves promoting communication between fathers and children in ways that enables feelings and views to be expressed in a new open way. This helps to clarify individual needs and desires and enables the expression of emotion, be it love, anger, or sadness. For one separated father the benefits to such expressive work and of attending counselling at the family centre he expresses in terms of what they learned about *him*.

> the fact that their father, they found out eventually their father was still there, he was never gone, he was only gone from the family home, you know. That I'll always still be there, although I'm not in the family home and I'm missing all those little moments that they're doing, yeah. But I'm still there. Everyone's always blind to something like. Sometimes you always need somebody else to tell you something. Plus as I said...they were allowed to express themselves.

The challenge for professionals working with men who have been marginalised through the courts /separation system is not necessarily to pinpoint where their anger stemmed from, but to intervene in the systemic cycle in such a way as to (re) engage the fathers in the most actively responsible way possible. That is to say, in a way which treats the men with respect, in a responsible manner, and which also assesses and where necessary develops the father's capacities to be a responsible active carer. We are struck by how it is only since we did these interviews and having analyzed the transcripts that we have been able to see the extent of the journey these men are on, in a way that it was difficult to see when the man was raging in front of us. How interesting it is that we have to get distance from them to hear what they are really telling us. This applies to all qualitative research, but seems especially significant when a lot of anger and danger is being expressed. We suspect that these are precisely the same processes and dynamics that lead professionals to close off to these men and not see beyond the rage. Reversing this is crucial so that vulnerable fathers, mothers and children may be helped to find resolutions to their relationship difficulties which will promote child welfare.

3.6 Working fathers

Fifteen of the men in our sample (63%) were working outside of the home. This is no guarantee of relief from poverty and extreme marginality in terms of such things as poor housing, crime and drug ridden neighbourhoods - the fate of some families in our sample. Generally, though, men in paid work were less socially excluded. Working men's narratives varied in the extent to which they saw themselves as active fathers, when not at work. Our data suggests that, according to their own self-assessments, father's levels of active involvement in domestic work and child care has certainly increased over time. Almost every man in our sample saw himself as more involved in these tasks and relationships than his own father was/is. Yet the most dominant pattern was for men to be the secondary carers, in the sense of time spent with children and degree of responsibility for day-to-day child care. We are anxious in saying this not to undervalue the powerful meanings that the paid work they did do 'for the family' and care they did provide, had for most men. For them, providing is what good fathers do, a crucial part of how they care. The passion with which some working men spoke of their commitment to their children made it easy to forget that they actually did not spend that much time with them because of how work limited it. What many of the men did convey was that every moment they did have outside of work was child and family centred. Equally, some men defined themselves solely in terms of their fatherhood role, even when that essentially meant being a good provider:

> *"It was probably, it was probably to work hard as well and to provide and to try. Financially you know, financially at that stage I, you know, I hadn't seen that there was a whole lot of difficulty you know with I suppose being able to be a father you know. I didn't see like, it was only later on that actually I saw that there was a lot more involved!"*

> (Philip)

This finding regarding the centrality of the provider role was common to all working fathers, irrespective of the degree of social exclusion. As the above quote shows again, men's relationship to their provider identities was not static, but developed over time with a distinct pattern of men (particularly in their late-30s, early '40s) becoming aware of a need to get more emotionally engaged in their family. Where there was also some variation in relation to providing was in the degree of necessity attached to work. All these men were desperate to work, in the sense of being driven to it by what the sociologist Max Weber called the 'whip-hand of hunger', and what it takes to materially provide children with a decent life. But the very poorest of families are driven by a particular fear of necessity, starvation and the struggle to give their children enough just to live a dignified life.

"I love working. I loved the job because it's so physical and what have you. [Wife] is at home full-time she doesn't work outside the home so I'm the provider paying the bills you know. So that's probably why I was doing all the hours and what have you, trying to keep the bills down and the food in and the kids happy. To have a few quid to take them out or get a video in and make enough. That's a pressure all the time, that's there, that's always there. Can you make enough?"

The danger however is that work can become all consuming, addictive and compulsive, cutting the men off from the family. As the same man relates it:

"When I was working up in the other place I was often coming in, I was often coming in at 12 o'clock at night or coming in at 5 in the evening and just going to sleep and then I'm back out at work again, just too much responsibility. And the responsibility didn't bug me what bugged me was I'd no time for me children. It was a 6 day week up there. The overtime wasn't optional it was compulsive (sic). When I did sign up first it was optional. They just couldn't keep their staff and what staff was left behind was getting more put onto them with everything I couldn't get off work."

Our findings suggest that acknowledging the heroic struggles of poor parents to provide a subsistence living for their children is an essential aspect of best practice with such families. This needs to involve 'being with' the family in their struggle in a manner in which they feel and know their difficulties are understood and being worked with in the interests of social justice, as well as support and healing. As one family centre worker put it, "we don't bring families in here to talk to them about how they feel about being hungry". Probably the single most important thing professionals can do to include working men in their work is to be sensitive to their work commitments, and arrange sessions to suit the father's working hours (Walters et al., 2001). Where this happened, the men gratefully acknowledged its significance and professionals clearly articulated the challenges involved. While men in jobs generally defined themselves as providers, some were struggling to spend more time with their children. Our findings suggest that what being a more active father means to men does not necessarily involve spending less time at work. The men and their partners knew that for the family's survival they had little choice about one of them being a full-time breadwinner, and for a mixture of cultural and financial reasons it tended to be the men. Being a more active father denotes rather a greater commitment to spending quality time with children, being as involved as possible in their lives; and generally taking responsibility for their welfare. Crucially, especially for these vulnerable fathers, it meant the struggle to be a safe, good enough carer and partner.

For some of the men spending less time at work and more actual time being responsible for and interacting with the children was a very real issue and an important symbol of how their were changing. Two key patterns emerged here. Firstly, where men were called to take greater responsibility, because they had taken over the primary parenting role from their estranged partners. Some men negotiated time off work (on sick leave) to settle in with the children, at the time when they took over being their resident parent and some established longer-term changes in order to see through their commitment to the children

I feel, I feel I've grown an awful lot in regard to that I'm not afraid to talk about my feelings now. I mean even work-wise taking a Saturday off that's sacrilege! Saturday is, that's [my employer's] Sabbath day. They make more money on a Saturday than any other day and nobody, no managers get a Saturday off unless you're on holidays. And I remember thinking to meself, well sod them! You know, before that I would have been, you know, frightened to go in and even to suggest that I might take one Saturday off. But I went in with the attitude, look, this is it. Like you know, I have boys there that need me. I have no one to mind them on

Saturday, I'm sorry I can't do it.   You know, I'll facilitate you during the week whatever way I can and make up the hours, but I'm not working Saturdays and that's it.

Having previously been excluded by the services because he was viewed as a dangerous man, this father became the primary carer for three of his four children (who were on supervision orders to the Health Board). For men such as this encounters with therapeutic and support services helped them to prove to professionals and indeed to themselves that they are safe and competent fathers. This included developing themselves to a point where they reached a new integration of the worker/provider and intimate self.

This illustrates a finding that came through in many areas of our data, that enabling men to become good enough fathers is inseparable from developing them as men and reconstructing key aspects of their identities and masculinity. Changing fathers is not simply about finding ways of equipping them with techniques to manage destructive behaviours, absences and acquiring better parenting 'skills' in some limited technical sense. In every case in our sample where significant change occurred, therapeutic and support work with the men - often in tandem with their partners and children - led fathers to question the basis of their identity as men. Gaining the necessary skills to be a good enough parent involves learning about the self, including the impact of how one was parented, acquiring capacities to communicate, active listening, expressing feelings, and engaging in 'emotion work'.

This is directly relevant to the second pattern from our data which shows men consciously beginning to spend less time at work and more actual time being directly responsible for and interacting with the children. It concerns working men who were the subjects of intervention to try and help them break old patterns of over-work/work addiction and neglect of a deeper intimacy with their children and partners, and with themselves. It invariably involved men in their late-30s/40s who's eldest children had reached their teenage years (there are also younger children in many cases) using social intervention to gain assistance with concrete child care problems but which, often to the great surprise of themselves, involved them in reassessing their priorities, 'finding' themselves and a space in their families.

This is typified by a father who initially sought help from a family centre with his teenage son's drug problems - "it's a nightmare, constant nightmare." But the focus of the 12 months of therapeutic and support work soon shifted onto him and his relationship with his wife. He was initially seen on his own for a couple of sessions, then with his wife and then for alternate sessions with the teenage son. The centre helped the parents and child to renegotiate their relationships, the couple to individuate, relax, and communicate better with one another. The father was over-working and drinking heavily.

> "I was having problems with [son], I was having a problem with [wife] because of [son] and I was having a problem doing the nixers [over-working] because the money was good and then I was overtired. I was like a zombie really."

He learned a great deal through the intervention work, such as how to

> just be normal. Hold each other, get out, socialize, talk more, share more experiences... [even] doing the homework, the housework and stuff like that, paying the bills. That's what I haven't been doing, I'm trying to work on that as well.

> I have, yeah, yeah, I've gained an awful lot. More, more into meself as well, knowing what's going on, and you know to try and put the bad things, things I was doing wrong get rid of all them, try and get them out of me system. You see drink was an awful, drink, it takes hold of you. You're a different person and I told [wife] an awful lot of lies over the years, drinking. And through drink and I'm glad I'm off the drink now.

For some working men it all becomes too much. Their bodies cannot withstand the physical strain any longer and they have to give it up. A crisis almost inevitably arises for such men whose entire identity has been so powerfully built around the performance based esteem (Real, 1997) they gain from the provider role. In this respect, again, our findings show that intervention work plays a crucial role in enabling such men to redefine their identities and make the transition from worker to active carer.

3.7 Mothers perspectives: Domestic gate-keeping and (re-) negotiated roles

We were keen to establish the degree to which parenting roles and tasks were negotiated in the past and present. Most men represented themselves as having 'fallen into' a pattern of roles and responsibilities, organised around traditional gender roles of women as carers and men as providers, rather than the couple having sat down and decided who was going do what, when. Significantly, one of the reasons that many men - and women - found themselves in need of social intervention was precisely because this tacit way of organising things was not working and they had begun (re)negotiating it.

The partners of the men we interviewed expressed a variety of views about them as fathers and their own lives. The dominant theme was a sense that intervention work was enabling them to re-negotiate roles and responsibilities within the family. Some mothers could hardly have been more positive about what their men did as fathers and partners. Working class mothers spoke vividly of the importance to the household of the family wage and in deeply honourable ways about the often extraordinary efforts the men made to provide it, invariably at huge cost to his physical and sometimes mental health. We learned too about the costs to the women themselves - and of course their children - of parenting in poverty.

> "Basically I'm saying poverty is an awful lot to do with it because the main concern is putting food on the table for their children. You know I mean like, the amount of stress mothers go on around here. It's very sad very hard for them, like umm, there are people trying to put the food on the table and that's a big worry, you know."

Given that, as we have argued, fathers were predominantly defined in terms of providing, this left mothers primarily responsible for matters domestic. Men explicitly recognised mothers as the gatekeepers of domestic work:

> No I wouldn't do housework. Well I'd clean up, I'd wash. I hate hoovering. I just don't like hoovering. I'd clean the dishes, wash now and set the table, I'd even make, make dinner. And clean up the room. Any decorations and the decorating I do.

> ... She's house-proud now, [wife], the house is spotless. I done the whole house last year because we'd a bit of a leak in the house, done an awful lot of work there.

> **Interviewer**: *And would you's have like worked out who's going to do what? Like, just talk about it like?*
>
> **Father:** *Well she'd say, would I do the dinner and I'd say yeah, I'll do the dinner. If she wanted to go into town, do a bit of shopping, I'd have the dinner ready there. Or she'd do the dinner. Mostly she does the cooking.*

This exemplifies one pattern from our data where the man's role was as provider and their account of what they did with their children since they were young was largely restricted to such things as playing with them. Crucially, though, it was precisely this kind of father-absence that was being challenged and re-framed through involvement with therapeutic and support services.

While one younger mother describes an egalitarian division of the domestic labour with her partner, she also clearly feels ultimately responsible and in control of what happens.

> *Well he'll do the cooking and I'll relax and I'll wash up after him, then he'll wash up after me. If we were cleaning the place I'd go upstairs and tidy upstairs while he's hoovering the kitchen. So we don't, like I don't want him to hassle me and I don't hassle him, we do, we share it, we share the jobs. We do an equal share of the housework and care. I'm the one that will get up and dress him, wash him, change nappies, make sure he's fed. But then again I get the day when I don't feel like getting up and Sean will take over and he'll do it for me you know. So I think the two of us would, like if he was tired now I'd just let him sleep on I'd just leave him in bed all day and say grand you know I'd do the cleaning over him. But this morning I did hoovering now yesterday, but today obviously he's at home so he'll clean up for me, wash the ware and hoover the place and tidy what needs to be tidied and that like. But mostly like if I go out with Alex once a week or twice a week I go and he'd stay home and he'd clean up before he goes out you know.*

Nevertheless the mother still sees herself as the domestic gatekeeper, with the man doing things "for" her, helping out. Our findings show that involving fathers more actively in family life can have unintended consequences, as it raises power and status struggles between men and women. While women generally wanted men to be more involved in domestic work, this was not without its anxieties and possible costs to themselves as they feared handing over some of the control of traditionally feminine areas to their partners. This often involved literal struggles over areas of the home, especially the kitchen, when men started to do more cooking - but often not in the way their partner managed things and liked. Thus, intensive intervention work, especially through family support services, focused on enabling couples to renegotiate gender roles and parenting responsibilities in ways which enabled women to 'let go' and men to find an 'intimate' space in the family (see, for instance, chapter 5).

3.8 The perspectives of children and young people

We interviewed 11 children from seven of the families. Given that our main focus was on fathers, it was beyond the scope and priorities of the research to interview a child in all 24 cases in the sample. We felt it essential, however, to include the voices of children in terms of reaching a deeper understanding of their perceptions of their fathers and what social intervention meant to them as children and any difference it appeared to make to their fathers and families. We purposively chose these 11 children as part of our in-depth case study approach through which we explored the lived experiences of a number of family forms, types of problems, social circumstances and interaction with service providers which were representative of the sample as whole. Thus the children related their experiences of a variety of problems and along a spectrum of circumstances, from relative social inclusion to extreme social exclusion and of a variety of intervention services and approaches.

The children relayed a range of experiences of their fathers and family life, which were without exception set within in the context of complex and invariably painful histories. Our findings support other research, which shows that children and young people are insightful about their own and their family's lives and able to articulate their views. All of the children we interviewed had experienced some kind of trauma in their lives, the most common being family breakdown and the loss of one resident parent and sometimes siblings. This invariably occurred on top of other traumas, such as domestic violence, that were a part of the family separating. Jason Dillon, for instance, was 10 years of age when we interviewed him in relation to the type of family support service he and his separating parents received from a family centre. Jason was eight when his mother and father (finally) split up. On balance, he felt it was now 'better' that they did not live together as he remembered they 'kept on arguing every night but then they were friends again in the morning.' He never really knew what they argued over since he would go to bed: 'I don't listen, I goes to bed, it was noisy.' He ended up attending the family centre because he needed to 'get cheered up,' following the separation which he found really upsetting. His dream (two years on) is still that his 'mam and dad would live together in the same house without fighting.'

All of the children we interviewed came from families where social intervention was connected to problems and levels of pain, sadness and loss which goes beyond the norms of most children's experiences. Our findings suggest that as part of developing social supports and intervention services, that actively engage with children, workers need to act as conversational coaches, facilitating young people to connect with, and express their feelings. While this applies to both genders, our findings with respect to developing good enough fathering show that there is a requirement to engage boys/young men in ways which develop their linguistic capacities in relation to emotional intelligence.

Jason's interview offered an example of how a child can become 'parentified' following parental separation. Being the eldest son, Jason became the 'man of the house' when his father moved out. With the trauma of the separation and the loss of previous security Jason began to worry for his younger brother that he 'might be kidnapped' and for his mother too that there might be a 'fire in the house at night.' Family therapy sessions at the centre helped to mediate the parental separation and to restructure the roles and responsibilities within the family. In addition to sessions involving all family members, the family worker offered herself as a 'sounding board' to Jason in individual sessions where he tried out with her what he might want to say to his parents. This all helped Jason find expression for his own sadness and anger: punching bean bags, drawing pictures and talking have all been part of helping him to find the courage to tell his friends that he now lives in two homes, something he still finds difficult since the boys still 'slag him about it'. Jason was adamant that the therapy had helped to ease the sadness that all of the family was feeling but that he had become the carrier of:

"I came here to get cheered up, I used to always cry because me da, me da used to get sad because we were leaving and he used to miss us when we went back to me ma after the weekends so me da or me ma were sad and I used to get sad about my da being sad and all. I wouldn't tell me da and me dad could usually see...I could easily see the tears in his eyes. And I'd know by me ma's voice sometimes [that she was sad]."

The family worker also supported Jason's father in finding ways to be emotionally expressive with his son yet not to 'dump' all of his own sadness onto Jason. Jason believed that the family sessions have been good for his father, helping him to 'get over his sadness'. Advice he feels all families going through a separation should be given is: "Cheer up and don't be sad and all that, it's OK don't be sad and it'll get better soon." This typifies how all the young people in our sample regarded a core aspect of best practice as facilitating communication between them and their parents, and between siblings themselves, and allowing them as individuals to express their feelings.

Louise (13) Samantha (11) and Roy Burns (10) spoke vividly of living in extreme poverty surrounded by drug pushers, suspected sexual abusers and violence from the community, or the continual threat of it. They attended the family centre for a range of reasons, Roy was being bullied in school 'for being a good student', while Samantha and Louise had seen a drug pushing neighbour threatening to kill their dog by shooting him in the mouth with a gun. The school had expressed concerns for Louise who was beginning to exhibit signs of becoming 'withdrawn and depressed'. Deirdre, the children's mother, herself had been assaulted in the neighbourhood and made the referral to the family centre. This use of a family support service exemplifies the negative impact on mental health, and well being of having to live in such dangerous environments. While the initial reasons for the referral were framed in terms of therapeutic supports for the mother and children, the centre went out of its way to include the father in evening time appointments and family sessions that he was only too happy to attend, 'never missing a session'.

All three children spoke about the positive effects of attending the centre. Louise, who had a previous experience of counselling, believed that what made this centre special was that 'they listened to you and didn't tell you lies' and that you could call into the centre 'whenever something terrible had happened.' Samantha commented on the way they always give you something 'nice to eat when you call in,' reflecting how the children spoke of using the centre as a resource that helped them to cope with living in such an impoverished community. For them, the centre had worked well with their father to help him relax after work, and talk with them more about how he was feeling. He was an extremely hard working man, who spent long hours out of the home, to earn enough to provide for the family's survival. While attending the centre Louise disclosed having been sexually assaulted while babysitting. She had not told her parents about the abuse and her father became really angry about it, his sense of failure to protect her from it and also her sense that she could not tell him about it. The family centre helped this father to become more attuned to his own emotions and to express them with his loved ones. Having listened to their dad talking in the family sessions Roy felt the hardest part of being a father was 'working', but Louise was convinced that the hardest thing for her dad was 'worrying about them.'

> "When your kids are upset or something that's the hardest thing, he gets angry because all them little things like out on the road where they throw stones at the house and they try and get Roy and beat Roy up so...
>
> When he gets upset he does not talk about things he just tells you that he's a bit upset at the moment and goes out and comes back in a minute. He tells us but my dad rarely cries, only once I've seen my dad cry.

The children believe that their father has begun to develop his capacity to express his emotions in a new way, something that their mother and the centre were helping him to do more of.

> "Like our dads not like other dads he's actually not because my daddy came from a very rough childhood and my ma actually taught him to love actually because his mother god forgive me nanny but she, she's very she's not like other nannies like she doesn't hug you she doesn't do anything like that so my daddy like he, he hasn't got

many patience but like he'll try and tell us that he loves you and all that and then he'll just walk away until he cools down and he comes back again when he cools down, but he'd never hit you he wouldn't."

Learning how to live a more emotionally expressive life is something the children clearly commented upon, yet when asked if there was anything else they would like their father to change they were clear that they loved him just the way he is. "I wouldn't change a thing about him, no nothing." Roy spoke of the pleasure of sharing physical intimacy with his father who wrestles with him in the evenings when he gets home from work.

> *"I love my dad. He always brings me outside and he messes with me like fight messing, messing and wrestling you know like. It's just getting close to me dad. Like when he's out at work all day we don't see him very much."*

The significance of professionals actually finding ways to include fathers in child and family work emerged as a key theme in the children's accounts. This was particularly so for those young people who were from families where a significant shift had occurred in the trajectory of the cases, from an initial period where the fathers were actively excluded from intervention work by health board social workers due to allegations and assessments that the fathers were unsafe, to a time where at least one professional began to involve and develop the men as nurturing fathers. Hugh (15) and the twins Victoria and Geraldine (13) had grown up living with a mother they all described as being unable to cope due to mental health problems. All three children (separately) described a childhood of violence at the hands of their mother who they alleged was also violent to their father, George. However, because he looked like a 'hard' man, with shaved head, tattoos and muscles, no one ever believed he was a victim of his wife's violence. According to Hugh, reflecting on their childhoods:

> *"My mam was young too like she was minding us kids all day and she was complaining about that and he'd [father] come home and he said she'd be nagging him why don't you give up work? 'but who'd bring the money then?' to try and support the kids and he didn't understand it. He told me that he just couldn't*

understand how to mind kids he didn't know how to change a nappy he said like he didn't have a clue he was only a young fella and she used to be waiting at night time with a bar like for him in there in the door she'd turn off all the lights and she'd wait then behind the door for him with a bar and swing it at him and try to like hit him she was fierce. She'd get fierce angry like and when she got angry then like she used to like swing bars and throw things round the house, break up the house and she'd hit him and you know that was the start of it like. You know what I mean it wasn't that bad then but like she used hit us when we were small she used to beat the shit out of us like she used to hit us like, lock me up in a place in all dark just leave me on my own and she used to hit us with wooden spoons and the a metal kind of a spoon like that she'd just flake at you when she couldn't handle making a dinner if she burnt her hand she'd lash out it didn't matter, if you're only two years old you don't know. I can remember getting hit like I remember that like and getting locked up in a place in all dark."

In part due to his father's sense of masculine pride and invulnerability it was not until the children's teenage years following a number of crises that social services became involved with the family. The children's mother took an overdose, and one of the twins, Geraldine, was placed in an emergency psychiatric ward following her refusal to eat, and compulsive washing of herself. Social services became involved following a referral from the hospital social worker who began the whole process of looking for a formal foster care placement for Geraldine. Her father George who had been caring fulltime for the other two teenage children was never even considered as a suitable carer, because of his appearance. Hugh believed that:

"He always gets judged by, you know, by his looks like his tattoos, his skinhead and his earrings and he like you know he looks tough like you know what I mean. I think that's what turns people against him."

According to the twins, "dad looks tough but he really isn't." Yet it was this 'look' that intimidated and prejudiced the social workers against this father from the very start, to the extent that Geraldine was very nearly placed in care. A new social worker took on the case and decided to assess the father's suitability to care for his daughter and she was placed with him. Yet, by that time Hugh had lost all confidence and trust in social workers and warned his father against talking with the new one:

> "He was talking to her and he said that this is the one and I said to him well it's not going to help I said because I said because all they [social workers] do is they go against us in the end they don't listen to us they side with my mother I said, don't trust them. Because they just totally side with my mother. From my experience of them, every single one of them, not one of them...you know what I mean...that probably didn't side with her the ones that I've experience with like that I can, that I know of that they were all...they all sided with my mam. So like I said to him, don't trust her [the new social worker] you know what I mean. But then [she] came up to the house then and she started talking to us and saying that, like telling my dad that he was good like and that he was doing a good job with Geraldine."

The fact that the new social worker believed in the father and told the children so enabled them to start trusting her. The girls believed that having teenage children herself gave this social worker the wisdom needed to support their family in a real and practical way. "She used to tell our dad not to listen to our bitching, that he was in charge, he needed that confidence that he was doing ok with us." All of the teenage children were adamant that what made a 'good' social worker was a willingness to listen to what they as young people had to say. Not all had this experience. Fifteen year old Michael Keane was on a supervision order to the health board and, almost ended up in care, " because there was trouble in the house and I was taken out and put up to my dad's for kind of safety reasons, because trouble was too much in the house". His father had previously been labelled by social workers as a dangerous man and unfit father, a view they came to completely reframe as the father came to be the primary parent. It had emerged that the children were victims of non-accidental injury from their mother with whom they were living. From the age of 13 Michael said he would lose control and become violent, "If something didn't go my way like" - such as not getting to watch what he wanted on the television. So far as he could remember social workers had 'always been involved':

> *I don't know how they started off, but the thing about the social workers is my mam organized all of them and she, it always seemed that even though I caused some of the trouble they'd always be on her side and I'd never get a say. I'd tell them what she did and they wouldn't listen to me and that's the truth because I think she got to say her story first, and I think that made a difference like. ... She'd ring them up and tell them everything I'd done and they'd talk to me about it and they'd know already that I'm lying because you know it sounded so convincing.*

It was against the background of feeling unheard and blamed for everything that Michael really appreciated the individual work that was done with him at the family centre.

> *the thing about [family centre] is I had a separate kind of a separate person to talk to and she'd [mother] no contact with him. And I found that very helpful because it gave me someone to talk to without them not taking anything in. Because that's what had happened with the social workers. They'd just talk to me and they'd know they wouldn't listen because they'd know I'm lying like.*

He insists that he wasn't lying but that, "they weren't listening", so much so that he described social workers as his "jailers". While blaming his mother as well as social workers for his troubles, he did not completely exonerate his father, although he regarded him as a good enough parent. He felt that this was how his father had always been and that social work involvement and a parenting course at the family centre had little impact as it didn't need to have. His father took a very different view, feeling that social intervention had enabled him to find the confidence and abilities to take full responsibility for his children (see also chapter 4).

This typifies how strongly these young people felt that social workers needed to believe men, and not just judge them on the basis of their looks or other assumptions about fathers which regards them as of little significance to children, especially compared to mothers.

> *"When I seen her [new social worker] and started talking to her it took me two or three times to talk to her and then I started copping on, she's sound like you know what I mean. She listened she listened to both sides of the story which was the*

main thing. She listened to me dad you know what I mean and she had to listen to my mother too. And she kind of saw what happened, she kind of listened to my mam and she was watching my mam you know what I mean, she kind of knew then that my mam wasn't like wasn't well. But she asked my sisters and me, which was the main thing that convinced us."

3.9 Concluding Remarks: Developing fathers?

Our findings suggest that like all men, vulnerable fathers have a capacity to develop through the life course. When social intervention does engage (well) with men, a crucial dimension of it is about developing them and their capacities for 'intimacy' as fathers and partners. This is an important finding and not as obvious as it at first sounds, given the very limited portrayal of fathers and intervention work in the literature. It shows how intervention is not simply about rendering men 'safer' or more responsible, as for instance, good providers. At its best it is about something much deeper and richer in how it helps men - as well as women - acquire skills and capacities to be good-enough parents and partners. Men differ in terms of their needs for particular kinds of therapeutic and support work, as we shall show in subsequent chapters. Our data suggests an important distinction between parenting 'skills' - in the sense of nappy changing, cooking, housework - and 'capacities' in the sense of emotional engagement, loving, equal, open communication. We fully recognise that the kinds of developmental intervention work we are referring to happens in only some cases and that many fathers are excluded from intervention (by themselves and professionals) and not made accountable or given the opportunity to develop themselves as fathers. But when intervention work does go on with fathers, our research demonstrates the scope there is for intervention work to act as a developmental resource for fathers and families, and the full weight of the loss there is for men, children and their families when this does not occur.

Chapter Four

This study shows that different kinds of intervention work are required with fathers and families, according to their particular difficulties and stage in the life-course. In child and family work a particular responsibility and challenge surrounds engaging and working with families where there is violence and abuse. Inevitably, then, child and adult protection formed a significant focus in this study. Our focus in this chapter is on the kinds of intervention work necessary with men and families where there has been violence, chaos, danger and risk. The chapter is built around two case studies which involve men who were in various ways, viewed as violent and a danger to their children and partners, but who were assisted through social intervention to become nurturing fathers. Each of the men are engaged in some kind of 'security' work as bouncers, 'working the doors of pubs and clubs'. Thus issues to do with violence, and the threat of it, pervades these men's working and domestic lives. They embody danger in other ways too, in how they physically appear, be it with muscles, shaven heads and/or tattoos. These cases show the capacity of men to 'grow' into the changing demands of what it means to be a 'good enough' father, evidencing the developmental, constantly changing multi-faceted and competing demands of fatherhood. We elicit from these narratives some key strategies for

4

Developing men who care: Violence, intervention work and the transformation of 'dangerous men' into nurturing fathers

engaging and working with 'dangerous men' and show how intervention work makes it possible to turn such men into responsible nurturing fathers.

4.1 Men, child care and violence

George Sullivan is 37 years old and lives as a sole father with his three teenage children, Hugh 15, and twins Victoria and Geraldine 13. He works as a bouncer and is a former boxing champion. George's story is of a 14 year marriage in which he was regularly beaten by his wife - here called Christine - who he describes as a 'manic depressive'. He related countless stories of her inability to cope with the children due to her mental illness, and of her violence towards both himself and the children.

> I'm telling you people wouldn't believe what I was going through, 14 years of it. When somebody's spitting in your face and pelting you with things and whatever and you can't do no wrong, you just start crying inside in a corner and say, who's going to help me, there's no one helps you. But my kids were often beat by her, thrown around the room, her tearing them by their hair, all because no one would listen.

According to 15 year old Hugh, when he was 'about three' his mother would 'lock him up all day long' and as he grew older would throw his dinner into the bin and leave him go hungry. His mother's 'controlling' behaviours and violence were allegedly extensive:

> It was everything, emotional and physical all compacted at once you know what I mean. I couldn't put a word like that, I'd say there's domestic and emotional violence. I'd have to call it both because there was physical violence and there was emotional on people as well. The thing is that like, on my dad, he was getting the physical stuff and then we were watching. We were all crying you know, our family you know what I mean, [my sisters] and me, my sisters, we'd be watching it then what'd be happening to my dad like and we'd be all crying.

Hugh also claimed that his mother tried to goad his father into hitting her so that she could use his physical strength against him in the knowledge that the police would never believe that she started it. According to George, his wife "controlled everything in the home, she planned the children, she picked the names, she wouldn't even let me make a cup of tea, she wanted to do everything." He used to go along with her, 'just to keep the peace.' According to Hugh his mother undermined all his father's attempts to involve himself in the housework. "No, if my dad done it she went over it." In their research interview the two girls, Geraldine and Victoria, made similar comments describing their mother as violent to their father and to them and Hugh, while depicting their father as non-violent.

George would have left Christine on many occasions had it not been for the children. His own family advised him just to leave, advice which highlights the gendered division of social attitudes to parenting, where 'any sort' of mother - even an allegedly violent and mentally ill one - was considered better than 'any' father at all. According to both George and Hugh, Christine's violence towards him had significantly reduced for about two years because Hugh challenged her when she was beating up his father. "It took my son to come in and stop her, he came in and stopped her. And to this day he's still with me, so it stopped her, no bother, he said stop it".

Despite such a chaotic history, it was only recently that social services had anything to do with the family, and after the parents had separated. Hugh was living with his father, while the girls were living with their mother in the maternal grandmother's home. However there were many arguments between Christine and her daughters which regularly resulted in their being thrown out of their grandmother's home and having to go to their father. George (and Hugh) believed that it was as a consequence of 'all of the hassle' that Geraldine ended up being hospitalised for 'strange behaviour', refusing to eat and compulsively washing herself for hours on end. She spent four months in psychiatric hospital and it was as a result of this that community care social workers became involved. The referral by the hospital represented this father as essentially a dangerous man, even though he was caring for both of his other teenage children. The entire direction of the case was to exclude him, until a community care social worker re-framed it, by going beyond the images of dangerousness to engage directly with the father and his daughter and recognise his capacities to provide good enough for his children.

Barry McGuire has been fully separated from his wife for a year and now has sole custody of their three children, aged 18, 15 and 11. He is 38 years old, a skilled worker and does some 'security work' - he's a bouncer - on the side. Barry and his family had been known, on and off, to community care social workers for some years, and to the family centre for about a year. Social workers initially became involved due to concerns about domestic violence, in the context of heavy drinking by both parents. 'Mary', Barry's wife, was a very heavy drinker and at the time of the research interviews was believed to be sleeping rough. Mary had reported Barry to the police and social services and, according to him, had him arrested for violence on at least one occasion, even though he claimed never to have touched her (on those occasions at least) and was soon released without charge. In his own words, they had become involved in a "tit-for-tat" scenario each blaming the other for family problems and involving outside agencies in their disputes. She reported him for physically abusing one of the children some years ago, which he confessed to, seeing it as excessive justifiable corporal punishment. She had quite recently, while drunk, rung the hospital where he did voluntary work with sick children and told them he was a paedophile.

He admitted to hitting her twice, on both occasions hurting her, framing this as self-defence, as "attacking back". His narrative was dominated by constructing her as the initiator of the violence:

> [She] hit me with anything she could find and would kick, punch. The thing was I should have walked away at this stage even walked out of the house on those occasions, but I stayed and tried to calm things down, which only made things worse on occasions. And I'm a big guy, [Mary's] only a small little woman, she's tiny. But she used hit me with anything she could lay her hands on, but unfortunately the two occasions when I did hit back I hurt her because I am strong. And I just lost it on a couple of occasions and I could have killed her, I could have damaged her. And I remember picking her up one day with one hand and throwing her away from me and she banged her head and it frightened me, it frightened me that I could do this. And it frightened me that one of these days if I didn't do something about it I would do something. And I had to, eventually I had to do something about it. I've spent the last year, year and a half fighting it.

He did not really construct himself as a victim of domestic violence as such, regarding the violence as a product of a very unhappy "tit-for-tat" relationship.

The family centre became involved at the request of the social work department. The centre's role was to work with the children therapeutically because of all the trauma they'd experienced over the years, witnessing extreme marital conflict, violence and a mother allegedly drinking herself into oblivion. There were concerns that 15 year old Janice had begun misusing drugs, substances and alcohol while 17 year old Louise had violent fights with her mother. According to the family worker the children would have spoken about "quite horrific violence between both parents. ...when they were quite young and they'd be waking up to violence, waking up to violent incidences, and how they dealt with that when they were younger. And lots of beatings and they would have spoken about having seen their mum beaten very badly by their father". They also "spoke a lot about their mum's drinking and also about violence in fact from mother to father but more of it actually was father to mother". The community care social worker confirmed that their involvement over the years was because of concerns about suspected NAI by Barry and domestic violence. Their recent involvement was to complete a court report regarding the family law/custody case, but not to provide an on-going service to the family. This was the role of the family centre to whom the social worker supported the referral.

4.2 'Dangerous' men, hegemonic masculinity and conversations of curiosity

As we have already argued, the most powerful reason why men are excluded from social intervention is because they are perceived as dangerous and/or unreachable. Connell (1995) has developed the concept of 'hegemonic masculinity' to account for the dominant construction of maleness that holds in a society. In Ireland the hegemonic form of masculinity which governs how men in general are seen, constructs them as emotionally unavailable, rational and in control, as 'sturdy oaks' who are invulnerable and have no need for or interest in being helped (Ferguson, 1998; 2001). This is not necessarily how men actually are. Few men can in fact live up to the exemplary standards and in reality there are a variety of types of manhood and 'masculinities'. As this study is showing, some practitioners are able to see beyond this dominant ideology of masculinity and engage men in their full humanity. Nevertheless, the asumptions about how men are, or should be, that are embedded in hegemonic masculinity have a powerful influence. Ironically perhaps, this is not necessarily personal as it affects how men are seen even if little or nothing is actually known about them as individuals. Thus, George Sullivan was judged dangerous and excluded as a father by a medical social worker, on the basis of his appearance alone without even having been engaged with. Constructions of hegemonic masculinity in welfare practice are heavily infused with notions of 'danger'. Potential male service users are not only seen as rational and emotionally unavailable, but as a risk to their partners, families and often to practitioners too. While these assumptions influence how men from all social backgrounds are perceived, they link to social class in a profound way. It is the most marginal men who are seen to embody danger and risk and are most likely be judged in this way. This way of seeing men constitutes what we will call a 'hegemonic fixation' which has to be worked through by professionals in every case.

George's first comments at the research interview were in relation to his shaved head, earrings and tattoos. He was a championship boxer and continued to work out and keep fit. Everybody involved in the case agreed that George was 'rough looking', including George himself who felt that his appearance often went against him. He considered that his 'looks' had more to do with the side of town he grew up on rather than an expression of his masculinity.

> *Being from the north side of the city I have tattoos, a lot of people would actually judge us by the way you look, cops especially and social workers, they take you on the way you look. People would say to me that I look rough and ready. There's people judging you, probably that's what's wrong with me like, there's nothing wrong with tattoos, I see nothing wrong with them. It's just that where I was brought up I got tattoos and whatever I don't know but I'm just caring too.*

Although it was some time since he had boxed George still embodied a very striking, formidable physical body. He now kept in shape by walking the dog and training Hugh who had followed in his father's footsteps, with his own success at boxing. Barry McGuire liked to work out as a body builder and by his own admission looks 'hard' with a bulked up physique and skinhead haircut.

These respondents inherently challenged the strongly held prejudices both of us researchers had in relation to 'hard man' life style choices like boxing and bouncing. We began by seeing these fathers through the lens of hegemonic masculinity, and relating primarily to the 'hard men' in front of us, to the exclusion of all other aspects of them. They scared us. So much so that when Barry McGuire explained that he was a bouncer in his opening account of himself one of us nervously replied: "I'm not going to argue with you then!". Even before the tape recorder was turned on he asked bluntly "what's a vulnerable father?" - a phrase he picked up from the letter of invitation to do the interview. This felt like a challenge, even though the reply was readily accepted. Our unease was well placed, given the negative public image of bouncers. In his recent study of bouncers in the North-East of England, Winslow (2001) shows how excluded men use their (hard) bodies and capacities for violence, often in connection with an underworld of crime, to create a new occupational opportunity. However, Winslow's study treats bouncers solely as public men and we are told little about what else is going on in their lives. They are one-dimensional characters, over-dosing on violence and control, the staple diet of traditional masculinity, albeit in a post modern context. The lesson is our acute awareness of how threatening it felt to be starting with a dialogue about vulnerability with what we were judging to be hard unreachable men. This is precisely what the professionals in our study tended to do by becoming fixated on images of dangerousness and hegemonic masculinity. What is needed then are techniques for getting beyond this hegemonic fixation to a genuine assessment of the man in himself and as a father.

In becoming aware of this, for us elements of the interviews had to take on the form of 'conversations of curiosity' (Cecchin, 1987) where rather than ignoring or denying prejudices, the interviewer actively uses them as a means of exploration and learning. The conversation takes the style, for instance, of asking the interviewee to 'please explain what it means to you to be a boxer as I have always believed it to be such a violent sport?' It is in working through these types of curious conversations that the possibility of getting to know the 'Other' lies.

The complexities of the men's identities soon became apparent. Barry quickly disclosed that his wife hit him throughout his marriage, although he did not regard himself as a 'victim' as such. As well bouncing, being a full-time worker/provider, lone-father and "a good dad", he did voluntary work with terminally ill children. This includes "sitting down with children and rubbing their hands, massaging their hands or their feet. .. I enjoy doing it for them and they enjoy getting it" and he is the only man doing such work for the organisation. He is aware of how he is initially seen by the parents of children at the hospital who "get a bit frightened" when they see a man with his appearance doing this, but he soon relaxes them and gets them to join in.

Rather than being primarily associated with indiscriminate aggression or violence, for both George and Hugh boxing was character forming, especially in relation to 'discipline'. They both valued doing it as an activity for shared time together. For Hugh it was his father's training and discipline in the boxing ring that actually got him through the most difficult times of living with the domestic violence:

> He's a very quiet man you know what I mean and I think what gave him that was the boxing you know what I mean, self-discipline, which I think helped him when he was getting hit. I mean he's used to getting hit, you know what I mean, he's used to getting hit inside the ring, you know what I mean so that was nothing to him. You know he said that's not new the getting hit you know what I mean you get used to it and he said she couldn't hurt him. I mean, because he said like, she was very small like she was anorexic like and he said like she'd be hitting him and she wouldn't be hurting him but the only thing she used to hurt him when she'd pick up weapons and she was dangerous. And you wouldn't know what she was going to do if she had a knife she could stab you, you know what I mean. She choked him, she tried to choke him but his neck is too big you know what I mean. She couldn't choke him you know what I mean.

Being a boxer also seems to have been George's access route into his job as a bouncer. He felt there were 'only two more good years in him' as a bouncer, the job ending for most men when they reach the age of 40. Contrary to reflecting a 'need for' or being drawn to violence, for George the rationale for this job choice was that it enabled him to earn money, and at night, so that he could be at home for his children during the day and evenings. Even during the time he and his wife were together, he claims he was a full-time parent.

He was working in order to provide for the children, rather than using work as a way of avoiding time with them. Indeed, even at the most dangerous and difficult times of the job as a bouncer, it was his focus on his love for his children that helped to get him through:

It's a hard way of making money yeah, do you know. I have to put things to the back of my mind, where I'd be, say on the door and I often worked on the door on my own and I'm nearly five foot nine. I worked in drug bars for years, they'd be high on drugs. I'd go in and I'd three kids at home, my wife was gone I was working on the door on my own. I was getting forty quid for it. I needed the money I had to feed the kids and whatever. I ran into a situation, I don't know they said your man is after starting inside. I went in trying to calm him down I know him personally. I know him so I'm down there on my tod [own] on a Sunday night. Fuck it I said, is it nearly time to go home I said, look at you. It's the kind of job you're in so there I am anyway he starts inside with me. So I says relax, I says you know. He was after firing one or two things around the place and I said [name] relax I says, forget about it I says you know. I know he's high because I can see by his eyes you know. And whatever way he just turned he just turned, fuck you, he says you know, all this crap so he attacked me. I'm there on my tod, I says, fucking hell how am I going to deal with this? I started to grab him and headlock him grand, I got him down into a headlock, now there's people sitting down with their drink. I'm there with my kids in my head. I know this fella and he's after throwing a few glasses at me, you know he's throwing glasses around the place. He had a glass, so I got the glass out of his hand and I went and I got him into a headlock and he was strong because he was high on drugs, they get very strong. So he was lifting me, he was the same size as me but he was beating me off the side of the television unit. So I says, here we are my kids are at home so I said I'm going out of here. That's the way I had to think straight away of my kids. So I caught him by the throat and pinned him against the thing and I ran him out of the door, out the door and throwing him a few slaps, I had to, to calm him down. Grand then, he went off. I got into the car and went home, got the breakfast ready and continued on as normal. And even my girlfriend says it to me I don't know how you do it, but it's the only way I can make money outside working during the day, but with the kids I'm going to lose all that you can't win like.

Barry's motivation for bouncing is social, it gets him out of the house. He is convinced that despite all their hard exteriors, the bouncers he works with are "real gentlemen", basically sensitive men and caring fathers. Moreover, Barry insists that he is always emotionally open and honest with them, so much so that they constantly use him as a sounding board for discussing their personal struggles and problems. Barry attempts to sanitise bouncing according to his own caring ideology.

> I'm not a puncher, I don't look for trouble in any shape or form. I will deal with it verbally 99% of the time. But if push comes to shove I will do what I have to do, with anybody.

In effect, through engaging in 'conversations of curiosity' our respondents helped us to make sense of their tattooed, muscled bodily appearances and what activities like bouncing and boxing meant to them within their life-world. While in some cases there may indeed be links between these men's practices and violence, we were challenged to be open to seeing them as expressions of responsible fatherhood rather than as simply signs of protest and danger. This is the step beyond hegemonic fixations that all welfare professionals need to take.

4.3 Inscrutable masculinity, marginality, and the social isolation of vulnerable men

Traditionally, male identity has been constituted in terms of the classic binary opposition between the masculine and (repudiation of) the feminine. Being vulnerable and seeking help in the context of hegemonic masculinity are seen as signs of weakness ('sissy stuff'), a failure of what real men are meant to be. Barry McGuire lived this out in an exemplary way and it was fundamental to what kept him from seeking help:

> Because you lose control of your own manliness, your own masculinity, if you go looking for help, you know. The old cliché: the man is the breadwinner, the man is the hunter/gatherer, you know, the man is the one that does everything. But if he looks for help he loses a bit of that masculinity or manliness, he becomes a bit more feminine, to ask for help. So you don't do that.

His story is dominated by a narrative of trying to prove his (traditional) masculinity. He was always "a bit of a wild one", which accounted for his difficult relationship with his own mother as a child. His celebrations on first becoming a father at 19 (unplanned - "nothing in my marriage was planned") had less to do with the joy of bringing his child into the world than with having proved his manhood: "I thought it was great! I was going to be a dad, and it worked: I was able to make somebody pregnant! It was not a kind of a fatherhood thing, it was, I don't know. No I never looked at it like that at all." In this idiom, becoming a man is a negative achievement and defined in terms of loss and what men should attempt not to be (Real, 1997). Thus for Barry:

> *I was always in control of everything in my life. ... if I let go of that control I was lost. I had to be the one that made the decisions, that took care of everything and made sure things happened. And it didn't go that way in the end and I had to start admitting that I couldn't, that's how I felt, I couldn't believe that I had lost. I'd lost and I could never take failure. I'm not very good at losing and failure to me was a subject I wouldn't accept it.*

Men's feelings of failure on becoming the subject of social intervention and having to let go of something precious, to how they see themselves is an important message from this research. Professionals need to be alert to this, and openly engage men about it and what they stand to gain. Men resist this even when the problems in their lives are intolerable, but they present a quite different face to the world. As Barry McGuire put it in relation to the violence in his marriage:

> *It [the violence] demeans you. I used to feel very small, I thought, I thought I was a hard one of a case, you know. Take on anybody, take on anything, but no... The violence, I don't know, it just, it tore me apart inside. I never told no-one nothing. I wouldn't even tell my family, friends anything that went on at home. We never told anybody anything. When I went to work I was [Barry] the happy father, the joker, a bit of a laugh, the craic.*

. . . the paradox that men resist getting help most at the very time of crisis when they most need support

Robert Morrell (1998) has developed the notion of 'inscrutable masculinity' to capture the paradox that men resist getting help most at the very time of crisis when they most need support. But inscrutable masculinity is not simply a psychological condition associated with being male, it is socially produced. The poverty of such men, and the identification of them by the police and welfare professionals with a particular type of dangerous marginal masculinity, places the men in a structural position where accessing help ceases to be an option. Help seeking is resisted not merely because it would go against the man's dominant hegemonic definition of himself as an invulnerable, controlled, coping male, but because it is seen as a real threat and would only add to their problems.

The more violent Christine was the more cut off from social or professional supports the family became. What stopped them from seeking help seems to have been a combination of trying to 'save face' in light of being 'proud' men, not wanting to get Christine into any form of trouble and, crucially, and an awareness of the negative judgements that would flow from George's appearance and marginal status. As Hugh put it,

> *She'd be trying to drive him out of the house so he'd leave. And he wouldn't leave he just wouldn't leave, he kind of held in there you know what I mean and we all knew what was happening was wrong but we couldn't do nothing about it because if my dad went to anyone they'd go against him. They wouldn't help him you know what I mean he never actually went to anyone he never ratted on her like because my dad's kind of a proud man like.*

Yet this male pride seems to have been a factor in the continuing disintegration of Christine's and the children's mental health. Hugh remembered how his mother would often 'just break down' ending up in bed for days on end. Ultimately Christine was only hospitalised following a suicide attempt (overdose), which Hugh and George discovered. But even in responding to this crisis father and son did not want to call an ambulance for fear of causing 'a scene' in the neighbourhood, so George took her to the hospital in the car.

George never felt that his side of the story was or would be believed. On a number of occasions when Christine assaulted him she phoned the Guards to report him as being violent, and he was removed from the family home. The Guards never, ever, took his side of the story, which didn't surprise George, who felt that Christine actively used his appearance to her advantage against him,

> she'd be saying I was abusing her, hitting her and whatever but she was ill she was ill for years and I never knew it and a lot of people wouldn't realise that she was ill because she was, she was a great liar. Oh she'd lie away, she'd lie her way out of anything. She'd tell lies that I'm doing things and whatever. And if you were the cops and you walked in and you saw the small thin little woman and you saw a fella 5 foot 9, 5 foot 10 shaved head, tattoos or whatever you're bound to side with her. I wouldn't blame the cops at the time.

Even on the occasions when George did attempt to put his side of the story, the Guards still sided with her against him, removing him from the family home rather than trying to do anything with Christine. As a result George learned that he could not use the Guards as a support or for protection for himself and so he never sought help for her violence. He was often in fact barred from the family home and sometimes spent months - and on one occasion as long as nine months - living apart from, and not seeing his children because she blocked him. He felt isolated and was poverty stricken because of the double burden of working to maintain the family while trying to maintain himself.

This financial trap is especially difficult for working class fathers who can find themselves trying to keep up with maintenance payments, in return for their access time with their children (Sheehan, 1997). One of the consequences for unemployed and poorly paid men, is that the double burden of maintaining two households is untenable with the result that they end up living in accommodation that is unfit for habitation and overnight access visits for their children.

> I'd be away staying in flats the size of rat holes and you'd have nothing like you know, you'd fucking nothing you wouldn't get your dinner, you'd have no money

and you'd be there struggling along and you'd be cold in the flat. There'd be no heating and she's there in the house when you're working and paying for it and you'd be worried about your kids and if you'd know her you wouldn't know what she'd do like.

Hugh recognises that, contrary to the hard man image, there are many sides to his father, and was deeply aware of the costs that all the stress and keeping things in had for his father's health.

Dad's kind of a mix of things like he's very good like. Like he looks like the hard man and when you talk to him he's fierce quiet. He cares and like he's working as a bouncer so lots of people think that bouncers are the hard men you know but he's not as hard. He thinks he's like hard, that he can take a lot mentally but he's not as hard as he thinks he is because he gets sick like. Like dad suffers from a bowel, a bowel disorder comes on, and his bowels come at him. I mean very sick like you know what I mean. Shitting blood, he's on a lot of medication over that, he's on disability allowance like over it. He's disabled over it like it's kind of a disability like. And it's because of what happened all down through the years like, he said he didn't know then what was wrong with him like when he gets very sick he starts shitting blood you know what I mean. All the stress and worry and stuff I think that's what drew it out of him and when my mam left it really came bad.

According to the twins, Victoria and Geraldine, "dad looks tough but he really isn't." In fact Hugh himself, at 15, has evidently already internalised an ethic of inscrutability. He coped because he had to, he felt he had to keep it all to himself because there was not "somewhere else to go. We just had no one to talk to really." He tried to get on with things, by burying the difficult emotions, although "they'd always be in the back of my head". Both he and his father used their bodies and one of the ultimate embodiments of inscrutable masculinity, boxing, as a resource for coping, to 'train' their way out of feelings of upset, rather than talking with someone about their feelings:

I talked to myself, I just walked and I trained and that's what I do. I ride my mountain bike or I walk that's how I deal with things do you know.

[George]

I just like it. You can control yourself like if you're angry like. You can come up and hit a bag or whatever you know what I mean and it's good to get out. You know what I mean or mental problems like you know what I mean. Like when my mam and dad were fighting like that you know what I mean you'd feel, you'd be a lot more angry or stressed out. You know what I mean you go up and hit the bag and go up and sparring with another fella like and it just takes your mind off everything boxing. When you're up in the club, you don't think about home you're just so caught up in you know training, circuit training and you go out and do your run you don't be thinking about what's going on and you don't think about school like. You just completely forget about everything. So it's a good like it's good to mind yourself, you know what I mean?

[Hugh]

Hugh does, however, show sensitivity and signs of emotional literacy in the research interview, which may reflect, in part, the impact of the social intervention that has occurred in more recent times.

4.4 The challenges of being called into active fathering

For many of the fathers in this study a life crisis was often the challenge that called them into active hands-on fathering. In George's case it was his teenage daughter's serious mental health problems, coupled with the children's mother leaving the family home. In an obvious sense this was also an opportunity given that Christine had allegedly been violent for 14 years. For Barry it was the realisation that his children were suffering due to the domestic violence, and his wife's inability to care due to alcohol misuse. Barry McGuire's marriage was a traditional arrangement and he did little or nothing in the house or with the children. When the marriage broke up and his wife moved out, to his surprise, his parents or siblings did not rush in to help and he got little family support. He had a lot to learn: "really housework was not my forte. I'd paint, decorate, build extensions, plumb, do anything maintenance wise, make railings, gates, I'd build the bloody house, but not clean it! You know, that was me". Now he does "the lot", including still learning to cook. "I still have days when I go Jesus, what have I put myself in for here? But no. I know I'm a good dad, as good as any mother".

Not having to put so much energy into a failing marriage has helped to free him up to be an active carer:

> because I'm let do it now the way I want to do it. ... without having to watch somebody else, without having to say look at somebody else's problems. I'm looking after me, I'm responsible for me, I'm responsible for my kids, and I'm the only one I have. I'm the only one. Again, now if I need help, I will go and get it.

George recognised that in the early part of his marriage he did not do housework or cooking. He saw his role as being a good provider, working long days late into the evening while Christine took all the domestic responsibility. The more mental health problems his wife experienced, the more he found himself doing at home, partly as a way to be there to protect the children. He had a lot of learning to do, as Hugh put it, "He told me that he just couldn't understand how to mind kids, he didn't know how to change a nappy. He said like he didn't have a clue".

Now George always feels challenged by the demands of domestic work and child care, which relates partly to his normative construction of gender roles:

> You know being a father's a very hard job especially when you're on your own. Women find it easier than men to cope with kids like they can do 3 or 4 things at once. I don't know you see I'd have to do the one thing at a time like put out the washing. I find it awkward like where I'd see (girlfriend) she'll do the cooking and ironing and she'll do the washing all together you know what I'm trying to say. Where I don't know, it's something passed down the genes, I can't understand it. But they can do more things at once, where men can't like you know. But I do find it hard, Jesus.

While George finds managing the housework hard, at the same time he sees his doing things for his children as being an expression of his love for them.

> *But I love, I love the three kids like, Jesus if they went in the morning I'd go mad you know. I love doing things for them, like I love, I love going out with Hugh to the boxing now and the girls Jesus, even if it's talking about the way they want their bedroom done up you know. They're into doing up their room now. This is the thing now, they don't like the colour on their own room. I'll do that for Christmas for them you know, I'll do it. I'll paint the room and I'm not saying anything to them because I'll surprise them, the twins.*

George was acutely conscious of his own vulnerability in living with, and caring for, young teenage women. Geraldine was continuously washing herself and refusing to leave the shower for hours on end. Actively intervening in the cycle of this behaviour necessitated involving himself in quite an intimate way with his naked daughter in the bathroom. This heightened awareness of the 'risk' involved in being a male carer for his teenage daughters, was influenced by his previous experiences of 'false' accusations of domestic violence which had been believed due to perceptions of him:

> *The problem was I had no one to talk to and I mean I'd no one, d'you know. I couldn't talk to anybody to ask them for help. I had no girlfriend at the time or whatever. The girl I was going out with I wasn't going to drag her into it. I was trying to deal with it myself as I always do. Jesus, I don't know how I got there. I just went day by day with it and don't know how I got there.*

Thus help-seeking even on behalf of his distressed daughter ceased to be an option for fear that he would be judged an unsafe and not good enough carer.

4.5 The construction of men in child welfare referrals

According to the community care social worker in George Sullivan's case, the initial referral from the hospital social worker was constructed as a child protection case and her role was to organise an alternative care placement for Geraldine, initially exploring the option of relative care. This arose from the demonisation of the father and how the mother (due to mental health problems) was for the first time in 14 years recognised as 'unable' to care for her daughter. As the community care social worker observed:

> Dad wasn't in the picture. Mum had given a very bad account of dad and said that he was very abusive to her, that he had been violent toward her and really he wouldn't be any fit parent really for the girls. I spoke to a social worker in the hospital who was very much against dad. Like he looks you know, he has the tattoos, the shaved head you know and I think she just felt you know on presentation alone that he just was like you know we won't even go there.

The 'truth' of the allegations about George's violence were never verified by the hospital social worker, who was prejudiced against him without any assessment of the father's side of the story, or his ability to offer safe care of his children. A case conference had even been arranged to try to organise appropriate foster care. It was not until the possibilities of relative care were exhausted that even the community care social worker considered George as a possible carer of his own daughter. It was actually Geraldine herself who suggested it:

> I went to the hospital to visit Geraldine, I asked her what she would like, what would she like to happen and she said she was anxious about going home to her mum. She wasn't sure that that was the best place for her to be. She mentioned the uncle that we had been with and I was honest with her and said you know ... that wasn't open to us and then she said well what about my dad? So I said OK we'll have a look and we'll see.

The social worker made contact with the father:

> I had the history from mum that he was you know abusive, that he was violent towards her and I had the presentation from the hospital that he had tattoos and a skinhead and you know maybe like we shouldn't be looking at him you know. But

I still felt look, I have the case and I need to see for myself that whether this is OK or not. Whether we can you know go with this man or exclude him, right? So at that stage I rang dad and I asked him if he could come into meet me and we'd discuss what we were going to do with Geraldine and in he arrived. And he was rough looking, he did have the tattoos and he did have the skinhead and he came in and we started talking and I said, I told him what I was thinking about you know, that I was thinking that our options were either him or foster care. And he was very taken aback I think at that stage d'you know and angry. And he said to me you know, everything isn't as it appears, you know I'm not the bad guy here.

The social worker did not get a feeling or a sense of him as being violent. She also met with Christine whose story she felt just did not seem to always fit. Some of Christine's extended family also spoke well of George as a father and significantly he was already caring for both Hugh and Victoria without any concerns being raised about their safety. She felt George showed genuine concern about the erratic nature of the previous care of the girls. George was invited to the case conference, but didn't attend as he did not want to be in the same room as his (ex) wife. At the conference Christine signed the voluntary care forms but George could not bring himself to place his daughter in care. He told the social worker, "I'll take her home if I can have support. I'll do the best I can. And we'll see how it goes. So that's what happened."

Barry felt that even once he had accessed help, being a man made a difference to the response he got from social services, as "a guy as well I was left a little bit to fend for yourself". He was critical of social services and positive about the family centre. He got little considered response from social workers, even at the time when he had battered his wife, and the social workers intervened. "And god knows, anything can be going on in people's houses, you know, unless the people chase them themselves". He spoke of a community care social work system that is perceived to be in great difficulty, without the resources to offer help even to those who want it. But what the family centre has offered has changed his life.

Barry's narrative is now dominated by a story of change and development, which is joyfully and triumphantly rendered, and in a manner that is now almost defiant in the face of traditional masculinity.

> *I would ask anybody for help now, if I think I need help. And I know if anything I'm more a man now than I ever was, much more in every shape and form. It doesn't bother me at all. The more help you get, if it helps you, it helps someone else.*

Barry has integrated an understanding of his vulnerability into his masculine identity. He has become a self-consciously vulnerable father, a shift he frames in the most positive terms possible.

> *Well, like I say, in the last couple of years, I think I've grown so much since I've got the kids and since I've got away from [Mary]. But I'm the oldest teenager on the block! I'm learning, learning so much. ... And the last 3 years I've been like a broken record. I've emptied out everything that was going on.... I still haven't stopped talking, I don't think I ever will.*

4.6 Beyond inscrutable masculinity: Fateful moments and expressive family support

Family crises, then, do not merely call men to take more active child care responsibility, they create what we call 'fateful moments' when the strategies surrounding the maintenance of inscrutable masculinity are no longer sustainable. While there is nothing inevitable about this as, crisis or no crisis, some men remain stuck in the inscrutable mode, newly self-consciously vulnerable fathers become more open to taking the risk of outside intervention and their relationship to help-seeking changes. This is partly because the men lack the skills and confidence to be able to carry such responsibility, and fear they cannot cope and may lose the children without support and also because more active engagement with children, opens up the man to emotional life and develops him in a manner which leads to a redefinition of his masculinity. How such fateful moments are used by welfare professionals is crucial to (inscrutable) men's development as fathers, creating opportunities for what we will call 'expressive family support work'.

George's recognition of his need for support was exemplified by his asking the social worker to be with him on the occasion of Geraldine coming home from hospital. The social worker believed that her way of working with all people was based on a respectful listening to all sides of the story. For George it was the social worker's confidence in 'talking straight' that made the difference. Initially, Hugh was reluctant to trust the social worker, fearing she would be 'just like the social worker in the hospital' and not believe or support his father. However he soon felt that 'She listened to the kids and she helped my dad':

> *She's a good worker like you know, a good social worker. She's good at her work. ... She just tells my dad kind of what to do with the girls, she'd be kind of like teaching him how to deal with my sisters and me like or whatever. Because she's a woman and a mother like she's confident then to go out and do it and that kind of helps him out a bit too like.*

George identified a number of key instances where he felt intervention made a difference to him as a father. These fateful moments can be seen as fitting with a 'generative approach' to working with men and fathers (Fagan & Hawkins 2001, Hawkins & Dollahite 1997). After so many years of problems, George's self-esteem and confidence were very low. The social worker not only listened to him but also told him that she believed in him, his story, and his ability as a father. For him, she offered 'official' belief in him.

> *[The social worker] said look Christine's after signing. I said signing what? Is she after signing her own daughter over? She said yeah. She says, you have Victoria out there you seem to be managing with Victoria, I said yeah. I said I've Hugh I says and Geraldine now might upset what I have going, I says so I don't know. I was thinking and thinking. So she says look the form is there look she says, there's one form there you can read it and that's grand you know to voluntarily sign over the full care of Geraldine. I was reading it down and I said fucking hell, I was speaking to myself like and I said, is this for real or what? And she says yeah. And she says well, what do you want to do? I couldn't sign it. I wouldn't sign it, no way I said to myself I couldn't do that. I'll go through I said to [social worker], I'll take a bash off it I says but I'm not going to sign over no way. How could any woman sign their own*

daughter away so I said I wouldn't do it. So I started crying inside there, she knew it then. [Social worker] knew I was alright. 'George I'm delighted', she said 'you're in', she said I always knew it. She said I said it to them, to the doctors and the rest of them that you wouldn't do it, that you'd mind them in the end. She had faith in me in fairness now like.

Moving beyond inscrutability to feel and express what is inside creates great fear and discomfort for men . . .

Expressing this 'faith' in George, based on his apparent capacity to parent his other two children, was significant for him in establishing his own confidence in himself as a capable and conscienscious father. The social worker continued this approach by praising and supporting George in front of the children during her weekly home visits, and giving advice which normalised the struggles of rearing teenagers, all of which helped to support Geraldine's re-entry into the family. This also involved the social worker in going into the emotional 'depths' with the family as they began to express a range of feelings for one another. On one memorable occasion she visited when the father was "exhausted and absolutely worn out from the fighting and the arguing." The girls "became hysterical" fearing their father was going to place them in care. Each family member ended up crying in a separate room and, as the social worker explains, she eventually reunited them with the father announcing:

I love ye. Ye wouldn't be here if I didn't. Now I won't let you go I won't ever put you into care but ye also have to give me a little bit and he said all I'm looking for is peace. And I just want you to get along and not to argue. And he sobbed and sobbed and the girls sat down and cried with him and had their arms around one another and I was just, I felt so privileged to see it do you know. I was sitting there going oh my god. I know without going two months down the line, I know that was, that's their whole step forward. The girls saw how vulnerable he was because I really think they saw him as the hard guy, the tough man, the guy who used to shout at them when they did something wrong. They thought that everything was OK for him. He had [girlfriend] and he had Hugh he didn't need them do you know. And they saw it they saw it as real as you could see anything you know. He said to

them at one stage, 'the reason I left your mother was for your safety, I saw her beat
ye and I was the one who held her back.' They both broke down as well and like they
remembered it you know and after a while everyone stopped crying.

Inscrutable men can appear inscrutable even to their loved ones. And breaking this
inscrutability down not only demands that they begin to let go of the control that has for
so long defined them and clear out the feelings they have held in, but that they are seen
to do so. Crucially, in not being afraid to take the risk of going after this man's feelings and
sitting with ('holding') him as he entered into the rawness of them, the social worker
managed to enable the expression of emotions that not only helped him, but began to
change how the father was perceived within the family and the overall direction of the
case.

Moving beyond inscrutability to feel and express what is inside creates great fear and
discomfort for men. In this moment George struggled with his sense of how he 'should'
have behaved as a man and apologised for showing his emotions, which produced yet
another fateful moment for the social worker to affirm him and a new kind of masculinity:

> *As I was coming away George said, Jesus he said, I'm sorry for being so weak and I*
> *said to him George you know tears aren't a sign of weakness you know as far as I'm*
> *concerned that's a sign of strength. And I told him, I think he's wasted, I think he*
> *should be in there telling other fathers and other men that it's OK to cry and it's OK*
> *to be and it's OK to make mistakes and it's OK to do, you know just to be. And as I*
> *said earlier on he's up there, one of the highest people I know.*

The referral for child and family work also created a fateful moment for Barry McGuire and
his children which the family centre used in a creative way. Initially, the whole family
attended, although Barry primarily wanted the children to be involved, it was "100% about
them".

> *...So I thought by talking to somebody else, if they couldn't talk to me, that it might*
> *help them as well, because they've been through an awful lot, they've been through*
> *so much.*

His wife attended the first meeting (at the centre's request), but then "drifted away and didn't want to be involved in it. She felt victimised, so she said." The family workers' approach to work with the children included Barry more than he initially expected. He liked their approach:

I was involved a lot, not all of it, but there was sessions where ... I was sitting down here and they were upstairs. It's very informal, that's the good thing about it. ... There's no kind of old time kind of, the old type psychology involved. It's very informal. You kind of sit down...they were playing games ... There was no kind of sitting there with pens and papers or tape recorders. They were able to just buzz off them a little bit. ... You know, and just let the kids say what they wanted to say. Listened. That's what it's about really at the end of the day, listening.

They didn't give advice. They kind of did it in a very roundabout way, which was great. You know, they weren't trying to tell you how to live or how to do this or how to do that, they listened. And they let you make the decisions. You know and I felt I enjoyed coming. I felt good about the people here, you know. I think they're good people you know.

So called informality and listening mean a huge amount to vulnerable fathers.

... It's the way they handle people. ...This is a very informal place, like a home. You're not being met as a surgery on the door kind of thing, or a chief psychologist written on it or it's not you know, it's not. When you come in here you're not talking to somebody that you are like talking to the doctor or talking to, you know. You're talking to normal people. People like that offer you a cup of coffee and you sit down and you can relax and you can talk about anything you want. It's relaxed. Now, the time slot OK, you know, you're kind of looking down, oops I've only another 10 minutes left. But, no like, the 2 girls I did work with, I, I only know [centre manager] a little bit. Again, I think more guys should be involved in it, a lot more.

These men point towards a style of working where they don't feel judged, can still make their own decisions, yet are challenged by the workers and indeed their children to change.

Facilitating communication between them and the children was central to the learning that went on for all concerned. Another example of such expressive family support was how Barry was confronted with his controlling nature and his "sergeant major" tendencies. The family worker's approach was to reflect back to the father the children's concerns: "So in family sessions then we would have addressed that with him and they were able to bring those things back to him". Barry really valued the sensitive way this tricky process was handled:

> *You know, they [the family workers] would say: would you say you're a loud person? And I'd know exactly what they meant, that the kids had said it, you know. But they didn't kind of say, you know, you shouldn't be doing that. They'd do it in a roundabout way, very good, much more approachable. Now I knew exactly what they meant when they'd say something...*
> *You don't feel like that, yeah, you're in trouble!*

Here again the inscrutability and 'control' of the man is inherently challenged as his children get to be honestly heard as well as seen. He too gets to voice his own feelings and concerns and is witnessed in that vulnerability. Workers 'hold' the family members together in a safe, trusting space that facilitates honest expression, listening and learning. Barry is convinced that the intervention work "did do the children good. Letting them "open up a little bit" and frames what he got out the work in a self-less, child-centred way:

> *I got out of it what the kids got out of it and what they were getting out of it. If I thought they were getting something out of it, it was making me feel better.*

He may have let go of something of his traditional need to control, but there is still some resistance to admitting to accepting help for himself. He can allow himself to be seen to be needy through the legitimate route of helping his children. His narrative embodies a struggle for men which Schwalbe and Wolkomir (2001) characterise in terms of the maintenance of a 'respectable masculine self', one which - in this instance - walks a fine line between the threat that intervention poses to the high value men place on values of rationality, and control and the opportunity it poses in terms of getting genuine relief with problems. Barry manages this threat to his self-identity through his children, framing the benefits of intervention in terms of meeting their needs, but still sees real growth and learning for himself:

> Me, I was able to learn, I mean at first they wanted me to go on a parenting course. And I said, no bloody way! I'm not being told, that's one thing I will not do. I will not be told how to, I'd try to change, I'm not going to start getting Dr Spock's version of how to be a parent. No, I'm not going to do that. I do it my way. But I will take advice. But going to one of these courses when they're telling you how to, no, no that's not for me at all. I think the way they did it here was much better. They gave you, you know, discreet advice, you know. For me, that's much better. You know. They let me elaborate on my problems, my own fears, my own insecurities. You know, poor me, they let me talk about poor me. You know. And I felt when I left here, I've got that off me chest!

This expresses well the balance of approaches this research suggests is necessary to effectively work with men, between practical support such as parenting courses and skill development and emotion work.

4.7 Concluding recommendations

These men's stories are compelling examples of how men can change out of a context of violence and trauma for children, and develop to become active, 'good enough' fathers. While both cases involved sole fathers, we believe that there are lessons here for intervention work with fathers and families whatever their living formation. Having to take responsibility for the children when their partners were no longer able to care was crucial to bringing them into responsibility. Clearly, however, the professionals still helped to 'tame' and develop the men in significant ways to enable their transition to a more intimate, care-based masculinity.

We are not suggesting that all suspected violent men are either not really violent or really nice lads underneath. On the contrary, Barry McGuire was by his own admission violent. The point rather concerns the necessity for professionals to approach the man with a 'not-knowing' stance (Anderson and Goolishan 1992), in a manner which acknowledges the multiple sides there are to men. The most effective father-inclusive workers in this study, who got the most positive feedback from service users, were those who were able to be aware of, and take seriously, suspicions of violence, but still be open to engaging with the man in a manner which does not prejudge him. As one family worker exemplified it:

not to be intimidated and just to basically to try as much as possible, I mean obviously to have a history of someone is important before they come in here, but as much as possible to put that history, you know, behind you as well, or just to allow them to come here with a clean sheet. [Female family centre worker]

The professionals working with Barry saw no problem with his being a bouncer and were able to work through any hegemonic fixations and go beyond danger, which is precisely why they worked so respectfully and effectively with him. The irony in social care is that even while such men display a vulnerable masculinity, or at some level are eager to, the hegemonic fixations of professionals means, they still tend not to relate to the vulnerable man. The corollary of this is that the focus then is on the mother, and often in oppressive, blaming ways (Scourfield, 2001). The key implication for practice is that a holistic view of men is required which explores and attempts to relate to the multiple selves that men are.

The analysis also suggests that a strengths based approach to such work is of crucial importance, where the father and family are affirmed and enabled to build on the positives they bring to their relationships and responsibilities. We recommend that strengths based work with fathers and families is placed at the centre of social care training and agency responses.

It also demonstrates the importance of working with children to heal the trauma of childhood maltreatment and witnessing of violence. While this has equal value for both genders, the analysis has shown the significance that intervention work has for boys and young men, in enabling them to go beyond the construction of an inscrutable masculinity to be the kinds of men that intervention has helped their fathers to become.

Chapter Five

Age is an important variable in assessing the needs of fathers and families, and the possible role for social intervention. Men at different stages in the family life-course tend to have different needs, problems and struggles, while each age group or life-course stage represents particular kinds of challenges for social professionals, calling forth the need for varieties of knowledge and skills. Younger marginalised men who become fathers are perhaps the most, at risk, yet invisible category of all. Typically, the position of men in public debates about 'teenage pregnancy' or 'unmarried mothers' is so absent and negative it as if the children had no fathers at all. Moreover, the implications of the (apparent) absence of those fathers from their children's lives is rarely seen as an issue of social concern. Nor is the fact that many younger mothers apparently have to parent alone, or at least without the support of an intimate male partner. At its worst, the underlying assumption seems to be that families are better off without such young fathers because they are invariably irresponsible and uninterested. In any case, it is women who parent, and all the social and cultural supports that do exist are organised around their needs.

Against this background, we were very concerned in this study to include the perspectives of younger vulnerable fathers, and their families and to investigate how they father, their relationships

5

Beyond 'protest masculinity': Younger vulnerable fathers and social intervention

with their children, their needs, interests, desires and what kinds of social supports and professional help can assist and develop them as fathers. Inevitably, given that the study in general needed to include vulnerable fathers with a range of problems and backgrounds, the numbers of younger fathers in our sample is small. The qualitative case-study approach we adopted provides such rich data on the lives of these fathers, their partners, children and the perspectives of the professionals who worked with them that significant recommendations for policy and practice can be made. This chapter is built mainly around two such case-studies of younger marginalised men, drawing from interviews with the fathers, mothers, and at least one relevant professional who knew the family.

Our findings show that, typically, younger fatherhood is unplanned. But this does not mean that it is (always) unwanted. On the contrary, the very marginality of the young man, the absence of other prospects in terms of education and work, can heighten the desire to construct a meaningful life, to see oneself as a worthwhile person and make a tangible contribution through fatherhood. The younger fathers in our sample went to extraordinary lengths to remain involved with their pregnant partners and form loving committed relationships with their babies. They had to, such was the pressure by family and professional agencies to exclude them. If a marginal young man in Ireland today wants to become a committed, involved father, with his children, he not only has to deal with the usual joys and challenges involved in making such a rite of passage - especially the adjustment to an altogether new form of responsibility - he has to overcome the immensely powerful pressures that exist to exclude him from his child's life. In most cases it is a matter of vulnerable young fathers remaining involved with their children despite, not because of professional systems. A powerful exclusionary dynamic comes from the state itself as the social welfare system creates a financial benefit for mothers to claim lone parent family benefit and for fathers names not to be put on the birth certificate, in effect for them not to be seen to officially exist. The paradox is that while officialdom generally fails to see the presence and importance of these fathers in their children's lives, in reality the men are active, committed carers, and seen and valued by their partners as such. Yet these young men also have serious problems, the most

Our findings show that, typically, younger fatherhood is unplanned. But this does not mean that it is (always) unwanted

significant of which is an unreliability which makes their consistent support for their children and partner uncertain. A core challenge is to move them beyond what Connell (1995) calls a 'protest masculinity' where their wildness is tamed to the extent that they can remain with their children and partners and in their families (as opposed to prison, for instance). We show that when child and family services do include such fathers, and do so in the particular ways that we outline below, the men and their families are able to use them to help them overcome some of the adversity in their lives to develop into still better, more reliable, fathers.

5.1 Entering fatherhood at a young age and in the context of marginality

Sean Whelan is 19 years old, unemployed and the father of three year old Rory. He became a father at the age of 16. Sean's partner Maeve is 19. Her first child, Jane, was born when Maeve was 14 years old and was taken into care at birth. Both grew up in poverty in families where their fathers drank excessively and were physically violent to all of the family. Maeve could not remember her father ever doing anything good for her, while Sean recalls horrific violence at the hands of his father, but also him doing good things with them. As a child Maeve was sexually abused by her brother and his friends, who were 'baby sitting' her. Maeve spent time in a psychiatric hospital because 'she was a nervous wreck'. Sean became homeless at the age of 14 when his mother and younger siblings moved into a women's refuge. Sean's exclusion from welfare services simply because of being a man began young. Due to his being over twelve years of age Sean was not offered a place in the refuge and so was placed through the health board in the care of neighbouring friends. However this placement soon broke down and Sean found himself living on the streets. He drifted into petty crime and served prison sentences. The couple met when Sean was 16 and Maeve 15 at the women's and children's residential unit while Sean (although in care and living on the streets) was visiting his mother. Thus Sean and Maeve's baby was conceived at a time when they were teenagers in need of services and supports themselves. From the outset Sean - at the age of 16 - approached becoming a father with a positive, responsible attitude:

Maeve told me she was pregnant and, ah, I told loads of people, I was delighted. Before Maeve got pregnant you know I always said to myself, I'm never having kids, you know! But I always said to myself I wouldn't take off and leave someone. I never would, Right? I'd never take off and leave her to look after the children on her own, like I'd always stay to help, you know.

Professionals, however, did not construct this as a case requiring a response that would include the (young) father in the pregnancy. Rather the intervention quickly became focused on working with the teenage mother towards having her place her second child in care, to the almost total exclusion of the father - despite his and his partner's desire for him to be centrally involved. The juxtaposition of Sean's commitment, and his exclusion by services is stark. Having a child was even the reason he had 'gone on the straight and narrow', the fear of separation from his child being the guiding force in his trying to keep himself out of prison, which could have drastic implications:

"So if I went away again [prison] what would it do to her [his girlfriend] then, you know. Eh, suicide then would be my only way out like d'you know what I mean? Then I can't go through with it because of this, [Rory] is the one that, that's holding me back. But I'm going to end up or I have a feeling I am anyway, but um, even, it's tough going like, just can't see another way out. Either prison or suicide like back up there like you know, I just can't handle it at all."

Significantly, fatherhood was seen by marginal young men in this study as at least one way for them to achieve something in life, in the context of a totality of perceived failures, in education, work, family relationships, crime and so on. In effect, committed fatherhood for such young men can be seen as a vital route to social inclusion. This makes the failure of services to understand, engage or help such men to meet this vital aim all the more regrettable.

Maeve was clear that neither of her two pregnancies were planned. She was encouraged by social workers to 'press charges' against the father of her first child, Jane, who was conceived when she was 13 and born when she was 14. This baby was placed in foster care

Significantly, fatherhood was seen by marginal young men in this study as at least one way for them to achieve something in life . . .

straight away, 'I wanted to look after her, but I couldn't do it'. Her mother was prepared to support her and have her and the baby move in, but her father would not. Having been put out of her own home by her father, she began taking drugs and alcohol, "to take my mind off where she [Jane] was. To stop myself from thinking how my life could have been, and how it was now and all this like. My child was gone."

Maeve's second teenage pregnancy quite easily confirmed her pejorative status as a 'high risk' young woman. She and Sean had only been together three days when she became pregnant, the first time he had ever had sexual intercourse. The immediate response of the social services was to move her 80 miles to a hostel for pregnant mothers in need of accommodation and support. The fact that this placement was at such a physical distance away from her home town did not arise so much from the scarcity of such services in Ireland, but the fact that it was strategically used by the professionals to actively exclude and get rid of Sean from Maeve's and their child's life. Maeve - who spoke well of the support she received there - saw her time in the mother and baby unit as her chance to prove to the social workers that she was able to keep and look after her second child.

I didn't want to go there but they all agreed, the social workers, my father everyone that I had to go there. You see they all [social workers] wanted to take him [Rory] off me. But then when I had him and I never thought there would be a baby that would be that small, do you know what I mean? So I thought to myself I'm not going to stay in [...] because I knew that if I did the child would be gone and I wouldn't get my chance you know ever to take him home with me. I'd three months to prove it to them.

Initially, Maeve's new address at the centre was kept a secret from Sean and none of the professionals ever spoke with her about him or the couple's plans.

He was trying his best you know, he was saying he'd stay by me now and, d'you know, he used to get things for me and the baby, he'd buy the nappies for me and he'd buy the baby's food for me and clothes for the child and he bought me the bottles for him.

Sean clearly realised the very difficult position Maeve was in and stood by her in her attempts to prove she was a good enough mother:

They [social workers] were going to take Rory off her, you know what I mean they'd no reasons now, they were going to take Rory. So Maeve said to me they're not getting him like Jane. Maeve was pregnant, like, as soon as he was born they would tear into her, as soon as the baby's born now he'll have to go into care and all this kind of shit like. And Maeve said in that case so she was after having Jane in [place], you know so she said if that's the case I'll fuck off like.

In a desperate attempt to keep her (as yet unborn) child, Maeve decided to make a run for it, with the active assistance of her own mother and a collection of other friends in a highly organised break out from the mother and baby unit. She was found and placed in a secure unit. This shows how child protection services can label such 'unruly behaviour' as evidence of a 'lack' of care on the part of the young mother rather than as a primal reaction to a very deep concern to care for her unborn child. She was eventually returned to the mother and baby home to give birth.

Sean was permitted to keep telephone contact with Maeve who felt "he was unreliable then. He'd ring me one day, and then nothing again for a month. Then he would ring me again." But Maeve believed it was worth trying to work through their struggles because "I don't want Rory to grow up without a father" and "I love him [Sean]". After a time Sean was given some practical support by way of one return bus ticket each week to travel the 80 miles to see Maeve.

I was talking to her constantly on the phone, every day like and I went to see her at weekends. Now I get a ticket off the social workers, they pay your bus, up there and back. So that was grand, I went up there on the weekends, grand like. But they only ever give you one ticket you know per week. But I wanted to be up there every single day like, you know what I mean? I didn't want to be apart from her at all. But that's the way, so we went through a bit of a rough patch because I suppose with Maeve just because you know she was so far away. ...We talked; she knew I wanted to be with her but there was nothing we could do about it, you know. We'd no money, no money to pay for bed and breakfast up there for holidays, we'd no money for that, we're not working.

Such enforced separations occurred despite Maeve wanting Sean to be as actively involved as possible in the pregnancy and birth process:

The best thing for a father is to be there, like I wanted Sean there when Rory was born. But then when I went into labour I tried to ring him from the labour ward. But then he was on the bus coming down to see me, when he got here all he said was 'why didn't you ring me like?' You know.

Sean did not allow missing the birth through no fault of his own to dampen his enthusiasm and love for his child.

I was well chuffed now, oh delighted. So, ah, that was magic, delighted with myself like. I'd a camera with me and all. I had the camera all that day like just using up film after film after film after film. Maeve, she was worn out like. Worn out. It was a long enough labour all right and when I saw him [Rory] first he was so small and everything I was nearly afraid to lift him up or anything. But one or two days later like I started picking him up and feeding him. It took me one or two days to get over the nerves.

5.2 Growing into parenthood

Sean and Maeve both wanted to be active in parenting their son together. However the social work and family support services still failed to consider this new family as a unit, deserving of recognition or support, and not a single discussion was facilitated involving both parents about their future. Despite the demonstrable commitment of the father to overcome the obstacles placed in his way, and the mother's desire for him to be involved, the case was constructed as a 'single teenage mother'. In order to prove her competence as a mother, Maeve stayed with Rory in the mother and baby unit for a whole year before she returned to her place of origin to live with Sean. Following the birth of their child even the limited practical support for Sean from the social work department diminished and he struggled to get a regular bus pass to visit his family.

> *I was only up there every month with the social workers looking for the tickets. I got them once a month. Instead of building it up they dropped it [visits/ bus passes] off. I'd be there saying to them when am I going to get the tickets? When will I get the tickets? When will I get tickets? I used to go into the social worker, but I used rarely see her you know, she could be behind the scene there, I'd say can I speak to [social worker]. They'd just say she's not in here at the moment and there was often times, there was often times when they said she wasn't there and I was only just out the door and I'd see her coming round into the office like, d'you know what I mean? I caught her then you know. I didn't get on very well with her because of that.*

They eventually moved into a 'cramped' two-bedroomed flat, and it was initially 'hard' getting used to one another. The effect of the previous year where Maeve was the sole parent to Rory and Sean a visitor to his family, had a significant impact. Sean felt that he had to learn much later than Maeve how to care for his son:

> *Because she, she worked through, went through it you know, she knew when to gave him solids and everything. I wouldn't have a clue. I'd just say I don't know what he wants or what I should do. Just like, she just adapted to it faster, more like, I don't know. But she was always always with him from the very start you know. I used to look after him alright but she was constantly living with him all of the time in [place] you know, like she was there since the day she was born. While I was only visiting them so he barely knew me for the first year.*

Maeve recognised how nervous Sean was about caring for Rory in the beginning but praised and encouraged his involvement as an 'involved father' (Lupton and Barclay,1997):

> *He's grand with Rory there and all, changing nappies and washing him, so in the beginning he'd be afraid if the baby was alright. He was afraid of dirty nappies but*

he got used to them like he changes nappies fine now and when Rory has a dirty one he says, 'I've a dirty nappy!' It is hard like when I had Rory first he was so small I didn't know what to do with him you know, the nurses showed me how to feed him his first bottle and then after that I was grand. But um his sister, he was living with his sister for a while and she had a child, you know and he used babysit as well you know he'd do baby-sitting. He's a grand [ie, good] father anyway now, when he looks after Rory I don't have to worry I know he always makes sure he has his dinner and he looks after him and makes sure he gets whatever. He takes him off to town and everything like. I don't know it just comes natural d'you know what I mean? It's hard to explain. You'd have to see him with him, the way he plays with him now and everything. He loves to play football with Rory and he takes him for a spin on the bike, brings him to the park, Rory loves the park.

Yet, our findings suggest that acquiring the capacities for active fatherhood is not simply a 'natural' thing. What this couple are describing is the classic pattern in how women and men become established on different developmental pathways as parents. While health, social services and family conspired to provide significant supports to help this very vulnerable young mother to learn to be a parent, nothing whatsoever was done for the father - other, that is, than sending him negative exclusionary messages about fatherhood. Our findings bear out other research which suggests that men's caring energy and desire for connection as a father increases dramatically around the time of the birth (McKeown, Ferguson and Rooney, 1998). By ignoring him, the services missed a vital opportunity - a fateful moment - which could have maximised this man's opportunity to bond with his child and begin to develop his capacities as a father (Hawkins et al. 1995). As well as his deep motivation and inherent ability to care for his son, this man's partner was a crucial resource for him as a mentor in guiding him into parenthood. She had the upper hand. His humility in accepting his need for support from her and their ability to pull together as a couple helped to see them through what for some are intractable difficulties, but this was not without its costs.

The wider implications of this can be seen in terms of how couples 'do gender' (West and Zimmerman, 1987) in relation to who does what in the home. Sean sees Maeve as the

. . . our findings suggest that acquiring the capacities for active fatherhood is not simply a 'natural' thing

primary parent, with himself playing a supporting role. According to him Maeve does most of the cooking (five days out of seven); she "mostly" cleans the house, and plays more with the children - "she just seems more playful than I". She brings the child to the doctor when he is sick, gets the medicines and so on. He does all the mending and fixing and fetching jobs, including going for shopping on his bike. His passion is for "Fixing push bikes, I love it. The one thing I do in the whole world that I'm good at doing. I've been doing it since I was knee high to a grasshopper, fixing bikes for myself, brother, neighbours, what have you." When he looks after the child his big worry is that Rory may get sick and he won't know what to do. For him, the most important thing a father can do for a child is "Love him, stick up for him like you know. Try and watch out for him you know what I mean teach him to go away from trouble". As for how he shows his love to his son:

I just take him in me arms every night, if we're watching tele like I cuddle and kiss like. When he's in bed I tuck him in and all, kiss goodnight and all this kind of stuff like. At night if he needs anything, more times I get up and I go to him, all that kind of stuff.

Maeve was more positive than Sean himself about his level of active involvement in household chores and direct care of Rory and paints an egalitarian picture of the division of domestic labour:

Well he'll do the cooking and I'll relax and I'll wash up after him, then he'll wash up after me. If we were cleaning the place I'd go upstairs and tidy upstairs while he's hoovering the kitchen. So we don't, like I don't want him to hassle me and I don't hassle him, we do, we share it, we share the jobs. We do an equal share of the housework and care. I'm the one that will get up and dress him, wash him, change nappies, make sure he's fed. But then again I get the day when I don't feel like getting up and Sean will take over and he'll do it for me you know. So I think the two of us would, like if he was tired now I'd just let him sleep on I'd just leave him in bed all day and say grand you know I'd do the cleaning over him. But this morning I did hoovering now yesterday, but today obviously he's at home so he'll clean up for me, wash the ware and hoover the place and tidy what needs to be tidied and that like. But mostly like if I go out with Rory once a week or twice a week I go and he'd stay home and he'd clean up before he goes out you know.

While not unhappy with his contribution, the mother clearly sees herself as the domestic gatekeeper, as unambiguously in control, with the man doing things "for" her, helping out. I make all the decisions about him [Rory] I always make them over everything like, when he goes to bed or what he wears going out like, or what he can eat. I know I'm right and Sean says fair enough.

Both parents believe that the most important thing a father could do for his child is 'to love him', or as Maeve put it, 'to always show his true feeling to his child.' Neither believed that a father's main role was to earn money to provide. While both believed that the mother was the 'real expert' and decision-maker, they shared an expectation that the father should do more of the disciplining, that Sean, in Maeve's words, should be 'more strict', playing the traditional disciplinarian role of 'wait till your father gets home' (Hogan, 2002). While she would never slap him, Sean would favour "tapping his nappy" to "show him, teach him like". For Sean this role of disciplinarian was the very aspect of his 'father work' that he found most difficult and stressful.

While it was not happening 'all of the time', their different approaches to parenting Rory was causing arguments and a strain on their relationship. Sean remained isolated and without any outlet to talk about or develop his own parenting style.

I just talk to meself there now, go out into the kitchen and start talking to myself like, fucking this, fucking shit you know, this kind of stuff, getting frustrated.

5.3 Men talking to themselves: The absence of social supports for fathers

"Just talking to themselves" is the position so many fathers find themselves in because they are ignored by services. Sean is explicit that

Maeve does all the talking to the social workers because she had another child you know, so she sees the social worker for that child. But there's no social worker all the time for Rory like, you know. But there's one there [for Jane]. ... There's one or two of them [social workers] calls, she has plenty of people to talk to if she wants. When they call like they say to me 'how are you like and how are you keeping' and all this like, but any details then about Rory or Jane, whatever, it's just Maeve and them. They go into a room on their own you know. Yeah. They'd be talking to Maeve. They never talk to me about being the dad.

If I answered the door at say twelve o'clock in the morning to the social worker they'd just say 'hi, is Maeve there?' I'd say she's in the kitchen, and I'd just call her, 'Maeve, the social worker's there for you.' And then the social worker goes into the kitchen so they can talk, in the kitchen, just the two of them like in the kitchen. So I go to them like 'how are you doing?' 'I'm grand.' That's it then, that's the only thing that'll ever be said to me then. They never said to you, would you sit down and talk with us or whatever or we'd like to talk with you, never.

For reasons to do with them both claiming social security benefits as single people, Sean was not meant to be 'officially' living with Maeve and Rory and claimed that 'the social workers know like but they said they would not tell on us.' However, he felt that his lack of official status as a father was related to the way he is left out of discussions by social workers. Yet Sean himself also contributes to his exclusion, partly because he himself has never really considered that he might have an important contribution to make to discussions. For instance, social services were considering allowing Jane to stay with them overnight:

I suppose I wouldn't mind being asked what I think as well like, you know.
... No, I didn't really think of it much before you know. I was just leaving it up to Maeve like when there are any social work meetings organised like to plan like kids in care, like reviews Maeve goes to that. But I'm never invited.

Here, again, Sean has constructed Maeve as the gatekeeper of whether he will have meaningful contact with social workers. Ironically perhaps, Maeve was convinced in the research interview that she would like social workers to include Sean. Yet she doesn't appear to have done much to try and facilitate it. This exclusion of the father, we want to argue, arises from two main sources: the powerful influence of social security fraud, and fathers' lack of official identity as fathers, which leads both mothers and fathers to publicly deny their role, and place in the family. And, secondly, the tendency for professionals to disregard fathers to the extent that they are barely seen to even exist. Even in situations where there have been prior concerns for child welfare, where the very integrity of the family and placement of the children at home is at severe risk, fathers are not considered - be it as a risk or a resource.

5.4 One-parent family payments and the social exclusion of (single) fathers

This couple were both in receipt of social welfare payments, Maeve the lone parent payment, and Sean the dole as a single person. They 'simply could not afford' to live off the one payment they would receive if they officially lived together as a family. The couple approached the allocation of money in a traditional way, with Sean handing over 60 of his 77 pounds income each week to Maeve - "I don't really need anything, nothing really, just fags". Maeve managed the finances because he was "no good when it comes to money".

Our findings show that the provision of welfare payments to lone parent households actually acts as a disincentive to the 'official' unity and integrity of families. In Ireland, most one parent family payments (97 per cent) are paid to mothers (McKeown, Ferguson, and Rooney, 1998). While this shows that the majority of lone parents in Ireland are mothers, and there can be no dispute that lone parents need a reliable and secure means of supporting their children, one of the central conditions of making the lone parent payment to mothers is that the woman may not cohabit. The direct effect of such a condition is to exclude both birth fathers and step-fathers who are in relationships with women on social welfare benefits from (officially) living with their partners and children. The lone parent family payment therefore is a structural impediment which can and does function to exclude fathers and undermine their role both practically (financially) and symbolically (as important if only in a bread-winning capacity) within families. McKeown (2001) argues that while the state has taken over the bread-winning role of the father it has done so in a way that supplants rather than supports the fathering role:

> In practice the one-parent family payment can turn single fathers into a risk to, rather than a guarantee of, the family income. Even the mother who is successful in getting maintenance from the father finds that, except in certain circumstances, the one-parent family payment is correspondingly reduced thereby making the father's net contribution redundant. Moreover, where co-habitation occurs with the consent of the mother - and is therefore technically illegal - the one parent payment leaves the father in a wholly ambiguous situation of living in a home where he is wanted but not supposed to be. For all of these reasons the one-parent family payment undermines single fathers and, notwithstanding its benefits to mothers, it is now time to ask if there is not a less divisive way of supporting single parents and their children in disadvantaged communities.

Sean and Maeve are one of the many couples in our study who lived this shadowy existence of being together, unofficially, in order to acquire a higher income from social welfare payments. They run the risk of being caught for welfare fraud, while Sean lives his life as a father being undermined by the very system of lone-parent family financial support in which he is complicit. The costs to him of this official exclusion are evident through all areas of his life. The complex systemic relationship between Sean's status as an 'unmarried' father (thereby having no automatic legal or constitutional rights to his own birth child) together with his 'unofficial' status as a (resident) father due to the couple's decision (on economic grounds) to claim two separate social welfare payments, played itself out in an array of interrelated social domains. This included: (a) his lack of official identity as a father which undermined his role - both financially and symbolically - in the family; (b) his exclusion from visits and family support work offered by community care social workers; (c) his (and the family's) lack of access to suitable and affordable accommodation; and (d) his lack of access to medical care and treatment.

The secrecy and 'official' confusion as to where Sean really lived played itself out in a very real way when it came to his trying to claim for the medical card that he was entitled to. Without a home address that he could give to the Health Board Sean found it impossible to get his medical card, and found himself going without necessary medical care for himself:

> My chest is killing me, I was just in agony like, pain, all this pain I could feel it all through my body. I used to know my old GP like, but I've only seen my new one once and everything, the antibiotics I needed were around a hundred and nine pound and I hadn't got a hundred pound, you know what I mean? So I just bought a few, four for eleven pound that's all the money I had to spare. I've no medical card I've sent away for it twice and they keep saying in four weeks to come back and that were nearly two year ago. If I could get the antibiotics it'll be gone. But I've no medical card I don't know how many times I'm after sending off for one and I haven't got it. The antibiotics would cure it but we can't afford it. I can't afford to pay a hundred pound.

In terms of their accommodation needs, because they are 'officially' two separate claimants they are by necessity defined as two separate 'households.' Therefore Maeve and Rory are given either local authority accommodation or 'rent allowance' towards private rented accommodation, but either source of accommodation is restricted to the needs of a single parent family, with the result that the living space is always tight and can often be a major cause of tension. The net effect of all these layers of exclusion for this young man and family were nothing short of potentially disastrous. Not only his fatherhood status, but the man's very health and survival is at stake.

This case study highlights the specific needs for support in such 'high risk' young pregnancies and births to teenage mothers and fathers. Sean's and Maeve's narrative of life as young people and then as young parents is one which highlights the continuity of needs and risks involved for children and families who live in poverty and social marginalisation. It could be argued that, notwithstanding these various layers of exclusion that Sean experiences in his daily efforts to be an actively involved and caring father and partner, he is the very variable that has made the difference in this young family, whereby Rory was not taken into care by social services. Maeve was both older and more secure and settled, yet she herself is very clear in her recognition that it was Sean's 'standing by her' that made all the difference. However, Sean was never included by professionals who never shifted from framing the work in terms of a 'young single mother' and her children. In fact the only part of the public domain that confers an identity on Sean is the criminal justice system, where he is viewed simply as a danger and possible risk to others. In the process, both the resource that Sean represents to his child and partner and the risk that his social exclusion represents to himself remains hidden from the gaze of professional services.

5.5 "One of the boys": Young fatherhood and protest masculinity

The second case-study of younger vulnerable fathers and families contains many of the elements of the first. What is distinctive about this case is that the father, Raymond Jones, was included and strategically worked with - along with his very vulnerable partner and their two children - and significantly helped by a family support agency. The main problem with the response in the Whelan case was not the provision of residential care for the mother and baby as such - Maeve Whelan was effectively homeless and sufficiently vulnerable on a number of criteria to seem to warrant such a response – it was the omission of the father from support and therapeutic work. What the mother and baby home provided was in essence a place to 'hold' or 'contain' the mother as she entered parenthood where she could develop her parenting capacities.

It was precisely this kind of work that was extended to both Raymond Jones and his partner Ann. Raymond is 23 and first became a father five years ago when he had a child with his ex-girlfriend and has maintained regular contact with that child. He now has two children with his partner Ann, Olive, 3 and Jonathan, 2. Ann and the children reside in a homeless unit for mothers and children, while he stays temporarily with his parents. By any standards Raymond relates a wild lifestyle. From the age of 10 he started misusing substances: "Drinking, smoking hash and taking tablets. Anything at all, sniffing gas and petrol". He first recalls getting into trouble for vandalism at the age of 5 and got into all kinds of trouble growing up, including injecting frogs with bleach, and taking, driving fast and burning out numerous cars. At 17 he became a drug dealer. He has served time in prison and is regularly in trouble with the law. He is a recovering alcoholic and heroin addict and at the time of the research interviews had been struggling to remain clean for nine months. "I don't feel 23. I feel about 30, 29 or 30."

He was "delighted" at the prospect of becoming a father, embodying that pattern where vulnerable young men see fatherhood as an opportunity to succeed at something meaningful in their lives: "Because the road I was going down, like I was saying, I can't, I didn't want to live like that no more you know." His ex-girlfriend became pregnant when he was 17 - he "never got used to" contraception - and he was heavily involved in all the pregnancies and births of his children. Even though he and the mother of his first child weren't even together, he went with her for "every check, every scan she had, yeah. I was with her all the time". He wanted to be at the birth of his first child but missed it, because, he believes, he was deliberately excluded by his ex-girlfriend's family. For him, "it's my right as a father to see my child being born, that's how I think of it anyway. Fuck sake, I put it there, you know". Unmarried father's struggles to be included are a significant theme in his narrative:

> I think women think when they're pregnant right, it's my child, my child. It's all my child, you know what I mean? And especially when they're not with the father. It's even more my child, that's what they're thinking.

Raymond and Ann planned their first child, Olive. Motherhood has changed Ann "completely. I was a wild child as they say. But I'm after settling down now though. I've no other choice really." According to Ann, she knew Raymond was an honourable man because of how he told her honestly when they first dated about his child and because of his evident commitment to the child. Her motivation was to have the baby so that she could hold onto Raymond - "I thought if I had a child by him that I'd be able to keep him". Ann was brought up mainly by her father as her parents separated when she was young. Her father treated her as a drudge - she did all the housework and care of him and her siblings - and regularly physically abused her. Her hopes for a partner were:

Well I was looking for somebody that would be good to me and somebody that would respect me and trust me. And I suppose well I do have kids like but at the time I was saying and if I did have children to, to want to look after them the way he's supposed to, like any other father would do. I just wanted him, you know, to love me. What he's supposed to do. And to respect me and to be there for me and the kids whenever we need him.

Now she "has him" she knows Raymond "wouldn't do any wrong to me". After her father, she just couldn't cope with another abusive, drunken man. Out of desperation she and Raymond tried living with her father for a time, but it culminated in Raymond beating her father up because of how he treated Ann and the children. It was this which led her to live in the homeless mother and child accommodation and get the intensive family support discussed at length below.

Raymond began to form a bond with Olive when she was still in the womb. "When he was there at home now if she kicked there inside in my stomach he'd be feeling it and he'd have his ear down to my stomach. He was, he was very anxious about her really, d'you know. He was delighted even when, d'you know, if she kicked now he'd go "your stomach is moving!"". As an expectant father:

He was, he was brilliant. He was better than I expected actually. He was, d'you know, he used come up to the hospital when I used get my scans and he used be all excited when he'd see the photography. He couldn't believe like that it was a baby he was looking at. His baby. And he used come to the doctor with me and when I was going in to have her then he came into the labour ward with me.

Raymond was present at the birth, which for him was:

Brilliant! Brilliant! Can't explain it like, I remember the time, the day, I remember everything, I can remember the whole day. D'you know, and the 2 of them. And there's a kind of a connection then with myself and Ann you know, a stronger connection because I seen the child being born, because if I'd seen [first child to ex-

*girlfriend] being born, more than likely I would have been back with [ex-girlfriend],
d'you know. I'm definite about that...*

The birth process created a 'connection' which affirmed his commitment to his partner and
awoke him further to his new role and responsibilities as a father. The increase in the man's
generative energy and desire to care for his child, and journey with his partner as parents
is palpable. Raymond's narrative is infused with a great sense of moral duty to his family.
By both his own and Ann's account he was an active father from the outset. He would
happily get up in the night to see to Olive: "I didn't care as long as I'd the baby in me arms,
then I was happy".   For him a good father is one who can

*Love them and be there for them. That's all I can do, I think. You know what I mean,
because they mightn't do the right thing, d'you know what I mean. That's what I
think and if he's man enough to put it there like, you know what I mean, if he's man
enough to put it there he should be man enough to look after it. That's the way I
look at it. Love, that's all they want I suppose. Money and all these material things,
you know, they're not going to matter, that's the way I think.*

He describes the experience of loving and being loved in this way:

*It's good I suppose, it's brilliant, it's brilliant in a way because I know there's some
fellas there only having and they're fucking going mad over it. D'you know what I
mean. And they're abusing drugs and they're abusing drink because of it like and
that's why they're going to jail and you know what I mean.*

In articulating his own joys of parenting he compares himself favourably to men who
cannot gain access to their children. His world view on fatherhood is heavily shaped by
marginality and feelings of insecurity and the risk of losing his children that comes from
having few rights. "I've no rights as a father because I'm not married". This is exacerbated
by his name not being on the children's birth certificates. The rationale for this is that if
his identity is officially unknown there will be less chance of them being suspected as
cohabiting. This again has to do with the couple maximising their income by creating a

situation where the mother can claim the single-parent allowance. Thus not only have he and Ann never officially lived together, his official existence as a father is further wiped out because his name is not on the birth certificate. In his experience all this gives the woman huge power in the relationship, which they are fully aware of. Getting the father's name onto the birth certificate is a crucial step forward he believes:

> *That's my suggestion, depending on the circumstances, on the man and woman who's having the child. If he's working, if he, I'm not a politician or anything, I don't know all these fucking politician words like, but I think it should be on the birth cert and a second name, d'you know what I mean, as a second name.*

According to Ann, Raymond is:

> *A brilliant father. Very good. I mean, he was there a while ago before you came up yourself and he was lying down on the bed with the kids and d'you know he makes up all his own kind of stories and d'you know things like that and he'd be colouring with them and oh he idolizes his kids, he do, even when he was away from him. I stopped the kids from seeing him and I was sorry I did because it made him worse, because he couldn't see his kids. And even his other child [...] he goes he travels to see her as much as he can like. ... He's very good with the kids. And they, you'd know by looking at them like they're happy children because, you know, they love him too and they love me as well.*

The impact of Raymond's absence from the children - such as a recent month long spell in prison - is clear for Ann in how Olive lost weight and was actually hospitalised because "she was very sick over him". She "was all the time looking for her dad" and has been putting the weight back on since Raymond's return. However, at three and half the child is barely speaking and is having speech therapy.

Their second child was not planned and has been more difficult to manage. It was then "definitely things started going downhill." Ann describes Jonathan's constant crying (for at least the first year of his life) as almost giving her a nervous breakdown and as almost splitting her and Raymond up. He feels that Olive is closer to him as she "can get around him", whereas Jonathan is "always fighting with him".

The big problem for this couple has concerned creating stability in their own and the children's lives. Raymond and Ann split up a year previously after they moved onto a council estate where he just knew too many people and was hanging out with them. Ann went off with one of them and Raymond gave him such a beating that he ended up in hospital. Raymond left town and started consuming huge quantities of drink and drugs "every night to forget about the kids". He returned to their home town after a few months when Ann said she wanted him back, but he felt she only wanted him as a babysitter. He started "heavy on the heroin" and ended up living on the streets for 4 months where he also drank excessively.   Ann said she would take him back, but he took an overdose and ended up at his mother's. She arranged for him to have residential addiction treatment and he has been (more or less) dry and clean from drugs now for about 9 months and attends AA. He did however go on a drinking binge just two days before the research interview. Ann, meanwhile, became homeless and was admitted to the homeless mother and children unit.

Raymond's overall estimation of himself in terms of his domestic commitment, housework and child care is that "I do me best like, you know. I do me best for them. You can't do any more". He conceded that he and Ann used to argue about this, "Oh, stupid things, you know what I mean, always over stupid things. Me missing all day or something like".

> Oh she wanted me to do what she wanted, d'you know that kind of way. Not what
> I wanted, not what the two of us wanted, but what she wanted. And fuck that, you
> know. Some days I'd do it just to keep her happy like you know.

Other days he'd ring the lads and go off with them for the day "For a bit of peace". He does not appear to regard his pattern of disappearing like this as significant. Being - or trying not to be - "one of the boys" forms an important part of Raymond's narrative. His ex-girlfriend (17) went off with someone else soon after she got pregnant, which "broke my heart". He interprets this as happening because he was trying to settle down into responsible impending fatherhood, he'd got a job and was giving up the drugs and drink:

just because I stopped being one of the boys like you know, she wasn't wanting to go out with me any more, d'you know that kind of way. So she just, that's why she wouldn't go back with me.

Yet, he never fully ceased to be one of the boys as life for him is a constant struggle not to act on his desire to do wild things, "Oh you know, all these fucking things would be popping into me head when I'm walking through town like". He does still get into trouble. As Ann put it, "I wouldn't even ask him any more because he's after being up in court so many times".

Excluded young men tend to enact what Connell refers to as 'protest masculinity', a way of being men - "one of the boys" . . .

Excluded young men tend to enact what Connell refers to as 'protest masculinity', a way of being men - "one of the boys" - articulated as a response to their marginalisation - from the labour market, education, the family. Men's practices of drinking, violence, and criminality together constitute a public acting out of a 'hard-man' image. Their status and definition of themselves as men is given meaning through protest, an acting out of being against everything that is seen as socially valid. Through interaction in a milieu of poverty and an ambience of violence 'the growing boy puts together a tense, freaky façade, making a claim to power where there is no real resources for power' (Connell, 1995, p.111). As Connell observes of the pattern, "There is something frenzied and showy about it." Crucially, however, it "is not simply adopting the conventional stereotype of masculinity" (p.110). As our data shows, these young men are perfectly at ease with non-traditional gender roles which involve attempts at egalitarian relationships with women and actively nurturing their children. Connell (1995: 111) recognises how this involves "a lot of concern with face, a lot of work put into keeping up a front". The crucial issue for social professionals is what to make of the façade – indeed, to recognise it as a façade - and what lies behind it? It is tempting to regard these young men as constructing a false-self system behind which there is no organised character at all, as evidenced by the periodic massive drinking and drugs binges and riotous behaviour. Fatherhood in the context of youthful protest masculinity constitutes a new challenge of public management of the self, how - or perhaps if - to continue to be 'one of the boys' while having to be for something, developing a new narrative of the self in terms of child care, nurture and responsibility. Our findings show, categorically, that the front that vulnerable fathers keep up to the outside world (including social workers) constantly belies the active, nurturing side of themselves that they may express in private.

When asked if it had significantly changed things having a baby in the house? Raymond Jones replied "Yes and no".

> Yes, with being quieter and being, d'you know, being more careful and more responsible. And the no side of it is just live like everyone has to live. D'you know what I mean. It's just the way, some things haven't changed much.

Raymond's re-evaluation of self even extends to questioning the entire value of traditional markers of protest and hard-man masculinity. When speaking of his "loads" of tattoos, he emphasises, "I did like them when I was a hard man that time. They're a sham like, so I had to get tattoos". Understanding the multiple sides to such men is important to appreciating their struggles and working effectively with them:

Interviewer: Some of the stories when I listen to you, you used the word, like being a hard man ... there's bits of your story that you know are really hard and there's other bits of you that are really soft, like looking after your kids and...

Raymond: That's the way I am like.

Interviewer: Which are you? Are you both? Are you either?

Raymond: Both, I'd say, when I have to be. When I have to be, but I don't want to be. It's not who I am, who I am is, I'm loving and different to that with my kids but if I have to be, d'you know what I mean, I'm going to

> protect myself and protect me family. That's the way I
> look at things.

The tension at the heart of domestic commitment and identity formation for vulnerable young fathers is, how to reconcile active responsible fatherhood with the enactment of a protest masculinity; the struggle between the caring man and the wild man. It is not, as our findings show, that the fathers are not good enough parents in their own right when they are with their children. It is the unreliable aspect to them, their tendency to disappear and be unaccountable that renders absolute trust and reliable parenting so difficult. The question for policy makers and practitioners is how to maximise the development of the nurturing man without denying his youthful, wild masculinity, the very fire which ignites and drives his passion to care and protect? In important respects, services don't have to do anything other than work creatively with the energy and passion that is already there. As we show throughout this study, the dynamics of love and intimacy transform lives, that "connection" that Raymond Jones spoke of on witnessing his partner give birth to their daughter. Ann, for instance, represented herself as a calming influence on Raymond, as tempering his wildness, setting boundaries across which she was not prepared for him to go, if he wished to continue being with her and the children. She emphasises how much she loves Raymond and it is her desire to see him stable and healthy, which led her to, for instance, recently warn him "don't even think of coming here because you know I won't have anything to do with you when you're drinking". Here again, just like with the Whelan case, women/mothers are constructed as mentors for (wayward) men. These narratives are classically gendered, in that, while motherhood is represented as having tamed 'wild' women, it is those same mothers who are also expected to do something similar with the rough edges of the wild men that fatherhood has still not managed to 'smooth out'. Even the women's strength is rarely enough, as the mothers themselves are invariably vulnerable and in need of help and support. In some relationships it is the man who is the reliable partner, making up for the mother's waywardness. It is not that the men do not ever give the necessary support, but that the need for strategic intervention arises when neither partner is ultimately stable

In important respects, services don't have to do anything other than work creatively with the energy and passion that is already there . . .

enough - in their own right - to hold the family together. Our findings suggest that the key requirement in work with vulnerable young fathers (and mothers) is to find a way of containing and channeling their energy and passion, of 'holding' the man in his family sufficiently to enable the development of his caring capacities and their triumph over the desire for protest. Even if social workers did engage with them, conventional casework approaches to such men are of limited value as a strategy for developing them as fathers. The most it can offer - a trusting relationship and advocacy - have their place, but these men, because of their marginality, need much more. The 'holding' of the men and/in their family that is required, needs an actual physical environment, a place to which they can attach, where the necessary concerted work can be done.

5.6 'Holding' and working with 'wild' young fathers, mothers and children

Raymond and Ann eventually found this holding environment in a hostel for homeless mothers and children. The agency policy does not allow men to sleep over - the unit would like to enable fathers to but can not due to the fact that families/women share some aspects of the living areas - so men must leave by 10pm. Aside from sleeping over, they now attempt to include the father as far as possible in all aspects of family life and the work they do with them. Raymond is clear that he was invited in by the agency on the very first day: "When Ann was going up I went up there. They asked me did I want to be involved and I said I did, d'you know". Crucially, in terms of a strategy for beginning to engage vulnerable fathers, the unit staff are very aware of the culture of deception arising from lone-parent allowances and actively work against it. They soon noticed a pattern where, with the mother having insisted that there was no father involved, suddenly a man would appear at the unit on a daily basis, yet, so far as the official system was concerned he did not exist, despite sometimes years of his partner's involvement with the Health Board. While recognising the fears of the women, they openly challenge the vested interests mothers - and indeed fathers - have in talking down the nature and quality of father's relationships with them and the children, and their tendency to minimise his presence in the family to social workers and other 'officials'. As the unit manager explains:

"And for all the fathers we'd have dealt with here it was their first time ever being asked to be involved with their kids in any structured way with professionals. We would know because we would be the only people who've asked them. We would always say to a woman referred here we would say have you got a partner? Is he involved? And is the plan to move back with him? Don't bother I don't care what the health board, what you're telling the health board, tell me what's really happening and if there's a father-figure involved I would say to the health board we're not taking the family in unless I can work with him as well. And that's what's happened because there isn't a point, there's no point in doing a whole lot of work with mum and kids, having her in a routine and then go back to somebody else who hasn't got that information who hasn't been in the learning process. And it's all going to be wasted."

The agency learned through experience that including fathers made good practical sense for all concerned if the work done was to have any lasting effects.

Ann finds the unit "brilliant. I love it up here". Although there because of major social problems, she does not feel judged by the staff. Rather, their approach is such that she feels affirmed in her parenting. The rules of the unit she finds "strict": "I mean they have to watch you ... when Raymond goes away by night I have to knock on the staff room door and say Raymond is going away. ... You couldn't do nothing out of the way and they'd know about it". She values the practical help with things like budgeting, which they cover with the couple together. Overall, Raymond feels the impact of the unit has been such that he has never seen Ann and the children "looking better". Yet he is frustrated by the fact that he has to leave by 10pm, which means he can't be as fully involved in the family's life as he wants to be. Ann also misses having him there as a support and for the closeness of waking up beside him each morning. He is, however, allowed to get as involved as he wishes during the day:

During the week, she's working 9 to 5 above and I'll go down to the crèche now and get the kids and bring them up to [the unit] and get the dinner on for Ann and stuff like that, it's grand like. ... [I'd] play with them and change them and give out to them and, d'you know everything a father should like.

The unit staff regard Raymond as an involved, committed father:

He gets on very well especially with the daughter who's the eldest of the two. He, yeah, he'd push the pram up and down you know he's no problems with that. He'll go shopping, he very much like wants to do things with the kids, have a bit of craic with them. And he does get on well with them. You know, they're delighted to see him coming in you know.

The value of such an intensive (residential) approach is evident in the opportunity it creates to help couples resolve disputes, especially those which arise when fathers do become more involved in child care and domestic work. As a family worker explains:

he's very into cooking, he has a background in [working in restaurant kitchens] and is very eager to do it. Whereas his partner, obviously she's lived, they've been on and off together ... she hasn't been able to rely on, she hasn't been able to rely on him. So she's very much in control of the kitchen, you know. It's her space. And she cleans up in a certain way and she, god, can't stay in the room when he's cooking because it'd drive her bananas. D'you know, so we've kind of worked it in a way that OK, if it does, then like come out and have a cigarette or something and let him at it d'you know. He, I think it's a way of getting him into being part of the placement because obviously if he's got to leave at a certain time he can't be here the whole time. I suppose he's going to feel he's missing out on something or he's not here the whole time. So the cooking is a huge part of it. ... and he loves doing it, d'you know. It's a way of getting her to relax around things as well because she's very into like, tables have to be cleaned down and pots have to be washed the minute they're used, you know.

The unreliable side of these fathers leaves a sense of total responsibility with the mothers, who then struggle to let go of control. Their belief systems, and internalisation of the oppression of being solely and ultimately responsible for the children, leads to tensions around the father being 'good enough' domestically, when he is involved. As this family worker spells it out: "she's finding it I think just a small bit hard because he is kind of invading her space. I mean this is, you know, her flat, her cooker and you know the way I tidy the room and she admits to that completely". Intervention work which helps the woman to let go of control and responsibility, and the man to accept it in a way which gives him a legitimate and trustworthy space in the domestic life of the family, is crucial to balancing the developmental pathways of couples, to creating negotiated outcomes in terms of gender roles and relationships.

According to the family workers, they have a good relationship with Raymond who values the service. "He's delighted to be here. He's made a couple of comments once or twice that he'd love if it was a complete family unit as in that he could stay overnight". An important feature of successful engagement and 'holding' of such service users is the capacity of workers to accept the multiple sides to the men and give them a fair chance. The Jones's family worker had learned:

> not to be intimidated and just to basically to try as much as possible, I mean obviously to have a history of someone is important before they come in here, but as much as possible to put that history, you know, behind you as well, or just to allow them to come here with a clean sheet.

Yet, a striking feature of Raymond's narrative is a struggle to admit his need for social intervention, or that it has had any positive impact. In saying this we do not mean to impose a requirement that fathers should appreciate it. The point rather is the lengths some men go to actively deny their need for help, even, ironically, when they are receiving it. When asked is there anything he'd like to be better at doing, he replied: "No. Why should I try to change myself for other people?"

> I don't know, well as far as I'm concerned I don't care about social workers and all these people. I don't care about them. As long as they know my kids are alright. And as long as they know I'm looking after them. Fuck it, you know, I don't care about them. Why should I? Not being smart or anything by saying that, but.

Ann and he would never have to ask for advice about how to bring the children up because "we know our kids, their personalities". He denies getting, or even needing support from AA.

All they do is make him feel better because he realizes some are worse off then he: "No I don't get support, but I listen to people and they're worse off than me like". Nor does he easily accede to having got any real help from the mother and child unit because he was okay to begin with:

Interviewer: Do you think since you've been going down to [the unit] you've improved as a father?

Raymond: No.

Interviewer: You haven't improved?

Raymond: I improved meself before I went, d'you know.

Interviewer: OK, what, OK, that's a better way of saying it: what are you getting out of going to [the unit]?

Raymond: Oh now I'm getting you. A bit of joy like, a bit of peace with me kids. You know. A bit of freedom like you know, with no one telling me what to do and doing what I want to do.

Interviewer: Would [the workers at the unit] praise you, would they notice things that you do and kind of?

Raymond: That's, they might, you have to ask them that. ... I don't be, I don't be looking for praise, you know that kind of way. I don't care, I don't care what they think.

Interviewer: Right.

Raymond: I'm not being smart...

Interviewer: No, go on.

Raymond: Once I know I'm there and doing what I am for my kids
            I'm happy.

The importance of illustrating this interaction, is it demonstrates that it is not simply what gets asked, but how it is asked/posed that matters in effective child and family work. Our findings show that fathers in general like a 'strengths based' approach which gives the man a chance to say what positive things he is getting out of fatherhood and intervention. As the above interaction shows, the father was much more prepared to openly engage when the interviewer changed tack away from questions which implied a judgement of the man ("have you improved as a father") to an open-ended positive oriented question ("what are you getting out of coming here?"). Yet his subsequent closure around not needing praise shows how even such strengths based approaches are never easy with men who are too proud, or conditioned otherwise to admit to their need for affirmation and support. Some men appear to need to enact a protest masculinity, to play out a particular notion of the invulnerable man, even while in practice they are receiving more help than they are prepared to admit. A key to this perhaps lies in Raymond's comments about the residential addiction programme he quite recently completed.

> *Oh, it was hard like, you know, fucking prodding and poking into your private life like and I wasn't used to that like. But I had to build a wall when I was on the street, I had to build a wall, you had to be tough. You know what I mean, because if you're not, you're fucked you know what I mean. Trying to break through the wall, it was hard alright.*
> *... they tried to make me see why I done these things.*

The personal resources needed to survive a lifestyle based on protest and self destructiveness, negate the skills and sensitivities that are needed to overcome and heal what is driving such behaviour. Refusing support and therapeutic help is not merely an ideological preference, but a visceral necessity, a requirement which is inscribed in the very ("walled") bodies of the men. Admitting to finding intervention helpful, is tantamount to admitting vulnerability because it concedes that there was something with which help was needed in the first place. For those men who don't wish to 'go there', other ways have to be found to engage them. According to Ann, Raymond "bottles-up" his feelings. So it is not just with social researchers that he resists being vulnerable. Yet he clearly is capable of talking very openly about his feelings for his partner and children. This has implications for practice approaches which need to enable men who struggle in this way to narrate about their children and avoid questions which demand an acknowledgement of too much vulnerability. In other words, the questions need to be strengths based and solution focused, centred on what he feels he is doing well with his children. Questions which focus on the men's deficits and failures will have them (or the professional!) out the door before you can say: "And just why do you have such a problem with ...?". A crucial part of all early work with fathers has to include assessing the man's capacities to do particular kinds of work, such as his expressiveness, emotionality and openness to being seen as vulnerable, and to design intervention approaches accordingly.

As we have suggested, something of this dynamic of positively re-framing interviewing approaches is evident in the above extract. Once the interviewer intuits the man's struggle with his approach and asks: "OK, what, OK, that's a better way of saying it: what are you getting out of going to [the unit]?", he begins to get a more positive response from the father. While still remaining cautious, the father responds to the strengths based questions and even goes on to disclose that the unit has offered him help that he badly needed:

As a couple now it makes us spend time, more time together and they say look if you want to go out now, we'll mind the kids and you know, that like, you know, which we'll do. We have a good laugh like. The first time ever we have a good laugh, well not the first time ever, but the first time for ages. Before it was a pain in the ass, everything was up in a heap, I was probably out on the streets drinking a bottle of wine.

Such 'holding' spaces need to be seen not only in terms of current provision in enabling people to cope, but for the stability and value they offer as secure bases for vulnerable parents to access if and when future trouble arises.

I'd be off the wagon, I would. I'd be demented again I'd say. ... It's a good place, more stable like d'you know what I mean. And then if they know you, you can call up and whatever like.

Raymond's hopes for the future are simple enough:

> *Well I don't plan too ahead, you know, too far ahead at all. I just, I just want us to be happy. I want my kids with me, you know, in a family home. I want, I want somewhere to live like I said a while ago, I just want to live ...*

And the unit staff are optimistic:

> *we are hoping a lot for this couple and hopefully it'll work. As I said, it's great to see the fathers involved but that's not always the case.*

5.7 Concluding recommendations

...understanding the multiple sides to such men is crucial to appreciating their struggles, and those of their partners and children in working effectively with them.

Young marginalised fathers constitute perhaps the most vulnerable single group of fathers, in this study, and in Irish society. We have shown the enormous pressures to exclude them from relationships with their partners and children that they routinely face. They are judged negatively and discounted from fatherhood and family life because of their social exclusion, and lay (especially extended families) and professional knowledge (especially social workers) of their 'wildness': the criminality, substance misuse, predatory heterosexuality and violence they enact collectively, with other men in public. We have characterized this, following Connell (1995), as the enactment of a 'protest masculinity' and the core challenge for professionals is to see beyond it if they are to actively begin including such men as fathers. Once again, this chapter has shown that understanding the multiple sides to such men is crucial to appreciating their struggles, and those of their partners and children in working effectively with them.

In a context of overwhelming failure, vulnerable young men can see fatherhood as an opportunity to succeed in a meaningful way in their lives. Promoting active fatherhood needs to be seen by policy makers and practitioners as a form of social inclusion. For this to be effective, our data shows the importance of actively involving young fathers from the moment of pregnancy awareness, at the birth and in the early months and years of the child's life. This helps the men to take on a fatherhood identity from the start and live out their bond with the child through shared parenting, rather than trying to fit in around the mother's dominant role. A core aim of intervention should be to get the couple onto the same 'developmental pathway' as parents. Intervention work which helps the woman to let go of control and responsibility, and the man to accept it in a way which gives him a legitimate and trustworthy space in the domestic life of the family, is crucial to balancing the developmental pathways of couples, to creating negotiated outcomes in terms of gender roles and relationships.

Our findings suggest that the main problem with vulnerable young fathers is not their capacities to care for their children, but their reliability and consistent availability to do so. Professionals need to see beyond the façade of 'hard man' inscrutable masculinity the father presents to the world, include and engage him in dialogue around his fathering and what he needs to develop. We have shown that a key requirement in work with vulnerable young fathers (and mothers) is to find a way of containing and channelling their energy and passion, of 'holding' the man in his family sufficiently to enable the development of his caring capacities, and their triumph over the desire for protest. Conventional casework approaches to such men - where they are seen periodically in their homes by social workers - have their place, but these men, because of their marginality, need more. The 'holding' of the men and/in their family that is required needs an actual physical environment, a place to which they can attach, where the concerted work that needs to go on, can be done. We recommend therefore that residential and intensive day care facilities need to be developed to work with vulnerable young fathers and their families, as entire units.

Practice approaches need to enable men to narrate about their children and avoid questions which demand an acknowledgement of too much vulnerability. In other words, the questions need to be strengths based and solution focused, centred on what he feels he is doing well with his children. A crucial part of all early work with fathers has to include assessing the man's capacities to do particular kinds of work, such as his expressiveness, emotionality and openness, to being seen as vulnerable, and to design intervention approaches accordingly.

It is of vital importance that the structural conditions which contribute so significantly to the exclusion of working class fathers are addressed. In particular we recommend that the father's status as a recipient of state benefits should at all times be kept separate from his identity as an (active) father. The same goes for mothers, who also have an economic incentive to claim the lone-parent allowance, omit the father's name from the birth certificate and effectively write the father officially out of family life. Mothers and fathers need to get the message from professionals, that how they choose to survive economically in a milieu of poverty and daily struggle is their business, but excluding fathers and denying children an opportunity to have an active father is morally unacceptable.

Chapter Six

As we have shown in this report, it is now widely accepted that the exclusion of fathers from child and family work is problematic and needs to change. Yet, a major deficit in knowledge existed in relation to how fathers can be included in intervention work, in terms of actual strategies, policies and practices. Against this background, the core research question addressed in this study was; how can more (vulnerable) fathers be effectively engaged with by social care services, more of the time? The aims of this study were fourfold:

- To document the needs and perspectives on fatherhood and family life of vulnerable fathers and their partners and children.

- To examine the factors and processes which lead to the exclusion of fathers from child and family services.

- To examine the factors and processes which lead to the inclusion of fathers in child and family services and to identify good professional practice with fathers and their partners and children.

- To identify best practice and develop a framework for policy and professional intervention with vulnerable fathers and their families.

6

A father-inclusive framework for family policy and practice

The preceding chapters have provided detailed analysis of case-study material which we hope enabled us to meet these aims. Our aim in this, the final chapter, is to draw together the various strands of the evidence we have accumulated through the study, and in particular with reference to identifying best practice with fathers. The aim of this chapter, then, is to provide a summary analysis of 'what works' with fathers and families and to develop a framework for policy and professional intervention with vulnerable fathers and their families, what we call a 'father-inclusive framework'.

A very important finding of this research is that promoting active fatherhood, especially in the context of disadvantage, is in itself a form of social inclusion . . .

We are aware that while extensive in scope, it was not possible for this study to examine all the kinds of child and family problems that involve fathers. It is important to emphasise that our intention was not to be specifically problem-centred in the development of this framework. We recognise that some types of problems - such as domestic violence - require particular responses which are tailored to promoting safety and welfare. It is not possible to cater for all of that detail in constructing a father-inclusive framework for policy and practice that can apply to the broad range of situations that professionals deal with - although we hope that the detailed case-studies presented in this report can satisfy at least some of the desire for such detail in at least some kinds of cases. Our aim was to include enough types of cases and intervention work to be able to develop a father-inclusive framework that is robust enough to withstand generalisation about how work with fathers and families needs to be accomplished and developed.

6.1 Outcomes: the consequences of including fathers

Unpinning any framework for including fathers has to be some conception of the consequences of doing so. This report has shown that 'vulnerable' fathers represent risks, and resources, to families. The best overall outcomes are those which maximise the resourcefulness of fathers. Our findings show how this makes for safer and happier father-child and couple relationships, that is families where the healthy development of children is promoted. It also has tangible benefits for men themselves and as fathers, promoting their capacities to care and experience the joys of relationships with children and partners. There is in turn a clear social gain from father-inclusive practice as our findings show, more involved fatherhood turns men away from lives of crime and self-abuse, which have economic costs in terms of health care, criminal justice systems and so on. Involved fatherhood generally connects men in a purposeful way to civil society and activates their desires to contribute to producing the kind of (good) society they want their children to grow up in.

Involved fatherhood generally connects men in a purposeful way to civil society and activates their desires to contribute to producing the kind of (good) society they want their children to grow up in.

A very important finding of this research is that promoting active fatherhood, especially in the context of disadvantage, is in itself a form of social inclusion. This is especially the case with the most marginalised young men, for whom we found fatherhood is seen as an opportunity to achieve something meaningful in their lives, in a context of loss and underachievement, in education, work, family relationships, crime and so on. The positive way these young men's partners portrayed them as loving, good fathers and the manner in which they portrayed themselves to us in interviews belied their public image as 'hard' unreachable men. Intensive residential work with such vulnerable mothers, as well as fathers, proved the most effective in producing outcomes which developed the fathers as responsible, fully available carers in the context of similar kinds of negotiated work with partners, and kept the family together. A core recommendation from this research concerns the need to develop residential and intensive day care services which can contain these young men, in their families and maintain the integrity of the family unit.

Our findings suggest that given the trauma resulting from domestic violence and child abuse, the most urgent and significant outcome of social intervention into fatherhood is, that it can develop men, from being a risk, to being an asset to their children, partners and significant others. The kind of detailed intervention work we have presented in this report shows that dangerous men, who have been violent to their partners and children are not only rendered 'safe', but can be developed as nurturers, and helped to become good enough parents. Effective father-inclusive practice promotes effective child protection. Significant positive effects are evident where fathers are not abusive as such, but unreliable and placing the integrity of the family at risk through the lack of consistent support and care for the children and partner. Similarly, significant positive outcomes were apparent for men who had lost touch with the emotional basis of the fatherhood role and who, while they were good providers, struggled with intimacy, and to make relationships with children and their partners 'work'. Intervention played a vital role in preventing serious relationship breakdown in situations where young people were misusing drugs and alcohol, for instance, by equipping the fathers with actual techniques to deal with such situations. But it went further in enabling these men to re-evaluate their lives and choose to be more actively involved as fathers, spending more ('quality') time with their children and partners. This illustrates a key outcome emerging across all types of fathers and families, and problem situations, in how intervention developed both fathers' practical skills and competencies at parenting - changing nappies, managing challenging adolescents, and so on - and the men's emotional capacities, promoting the kinds of critical self-reflection which led the men to redefine key aspects of their masculinity in the creation of a more nurturing self.

Mothers felt that intervention brought considerable benefits to themselves, by helping to produce men who shared parenting, and were physically and emotionally available to them . . .

The research has demonstrated the crucial role of intervention work in helping men to heal, especially when the men are survivors of trauma such as childhood sexual abuse. This has concrete benefits in developing their capacities to parent in the most intimate ways, freeing them for instance, to feel comfortable enough, as abuse survivors, to touch and hug their children. They were also helped to free up the emotional blocks and pain that led them into addictive and destructive behaviour, with the self and others, developing their capacities to be in equal, expressive relationships with their partners and children, to be in 'democratic families'. This reflects a key overall outcome of social intervention with vulnerable fathers, in how it connects with the healing power of love in (fractured) families. What we have called 'the restorative power of love' refers to how men and women can heal each other and themselves in loving relationships; where fathers (and mothers) can and do fall in love with children who are not blood related and how living in the love of children can heal some of the trauma that adults once suffered as children themselves.

Involved fatherhood benefits mothers as well as children. In general, the mothers we interviewed wanted the men to be actively involved fathers and felt that intervention work had developed the men's capacities to nurture and take domestic responsibility. Mothers felt that intervention brought considerable benefits to themselves, by helping to produce men who shared parenting, and were physically and emotionally available to them. It also brought benefits to mothers in helping them to develop parenting skills and (re)negotiate roles and relationships with the men. Our findings demonstrate a significant outcome in terms of how intervention requires (vulnerable) mothers, as well as fathers to change. Women were challenged and supported by professionals to see the role they had been given, and taken on, as domestic gatekeepers, and to create a space in relationships and domestic routines to let the men be more active fathers. Women had to let go their over-developed sense of responsibility for all things domestic, and accept fathers ways of doing things in how they directly cared for children, cooked, used the kitchen and so on, as good enough. This went hand-in-hand of course with calling the fathers into taking such domestic responsibility.

The benefits for mothers are perhaps most obvious where vulnerable mother's in-capacities to care for their children place the children at risk of entering Care or result in such action. At their most resourceful, involved fathers can contribute the kinds of support and nurture that is necessary to keep children in their families. This emerged in our data in a variety of ways, and especially in terms of the positive presence of step-fathers in families. Yet fathers as a safe, developmental 'resource' for their children, was far from a clear-cut matter in many situations, irrespective of family form. As we have shown, some fathers of children who were initially labelled as a 'risk', as dangerous and/or useless, were re-framed through social intervention as good-enough fathers and the primary, reliable parent. Thus the status of fathers as risks or resources does not remain static, but is apt to change as the intervention work interfaces with the ebbs and flows of the life experiences of families. Again, alongside the crucial emotional benefits of this for children, there is a significant social and economic gain in involving fathers as the State does not have to pay for alternative care for children.

Child and family work, by it very nature, involves relationship problems, trauma, pain and loss. The report has documented the crucial family support work that is being done with separated fathers, their children and (sometimes) mothers. Significant positive outcomes have been shown to occur for fathers in acrimonious marital breakdown situations, where custody of, and access to, children is being viciously fought over by warring parents. The fathers have been helped to deal with their anger at being excluded from anything other than minimal contact with their children by the family law system, and to find ways of having open communication with their children about their feelings and wishes.

Our findings suggest that, overall, father-inclusive practice has tangible positive outcomes for children . . .

Our findings suggest that, overall, father-inclusive practice has tangible positive outcomes for children. All of the children we interviewed expressed a desire to have close loving relationships with their fathers, and felt that in general this had been enhanced through intervention work. Children were critical of professional responses which they perceived to take one parent's side, usually the mothers, as this unfairly excluded their fathers and did not give them a chance. What children valued most - even if they often found it awkward and hard-work - was individual direct work as well as whole family sessions which included their fathers, and created opportunities for honest communication about feelings, and open democratic discussion which took account of their wishes in deciding and planning the future. Through such work, vulnerable families were helped to heal and 'move on'. Crucially, children as well as fathers were helped to gain emotional literacy and a more congruent relationship with themselves. Given the primary focus of this study, without in any way denigrating the importance of this for girls, we do want to emphasize the positive outcomes of this kind of 'expressive family support work' for boys. Our findings show conclusively that the more vulnerable boys are left to deal with their trauma on their own, as was the childhood experiences of all of the fathers we interviewed. The more they develop a self-concept based around values of 'inscrutable masculinity', and a closure around acknowledging vulnerability and seeking help - all of which contributes to them becoming vulnerable fathers. This report has shown the significance that intervention work has for boys and young men in enabling them to go beyond the construction of an inscrutable masculinity, to be the kinds of men that intervention has helped their fathers to become.

6.2 Key features of a father-inclusive framework

As we have shown in this report, while good practice is certainly going on, it is the norm for fathers to be excluded from work with welfare practitioners. An important finding of the research is that inclusion and exclusion are often not mutually exclusive experiences. Even those men who have been included by (some) services or professional(s) usually have experience of being excluded by (some) services or professional(s) in the past or present. The key point is that the exclusion of fathers is so common an experience, that rarely is their inclusion straightforward. Father-inclusive practice, therefore, because it is being developed in the context of such a powerful exclusionary impulse, requires concerted, focused action to include the man. The exception, as we have acknowledged, are those instances where the exclusion of men seems clearly justified because they constitute a real, known threat to the safety of children, women and/or professionals. Our findings however, suggest that even these situations can be less straightforward then they look, given that we found instances where men who were labelled as dangerous and excluded from the family and intervention on those grounds, turned out on closer examination not to be. The tension that practitioners must constantly wrestle within their work with suspected dangerous men, is to take that danger seriously, while questioning the basis for that judgement and its implications. By the 'inclusion' of men we are referring to a continuum of engagement which at a minimum involves talking directly to the man about fatherhood, the family and the problems at hand, and, at the other extreme involves in-depth work to develop him as a father. The most troubling examples of exclusion we came across involved the systematic discarding of men as fathers without even the minimum of engagement, such as a conversation with him. The father's official identity was based on his appearance, what professionals and other family members said about him, coupled with powerful tacit assumptions about (dangerous) masculinity and how men are thought to be. This is unacceptable. The risks that a man represents have to be very great indeed to justify his exclusion from intervention work and sometimes the family, without at the very least directly engaging with him.

In general, the inclusion of men needs to be done in a manner that engages him in the most open, honest, serious way possible, avoiding, for instance, trying to coyly entice him in through a focus on talking about what one social worker called "the nice things". As the fathers we interviewed all testified to, they are acutely aware of the serious issues in their own and the children's lives, and they need and deserve to be engaged with about them. To them, for professionals not to do so seems strange and irresponsible, an abuse of the power professionals have to determine legitimate agendas in child and family work. Yet, we also found that in some instances fathers avoid professionals. The kinds of fears men typically have of professional involvement include:

■ Going against a definition of masculinity which values strength, coping and repudiates vulnerability and needs for support.

■ being seen at all with the children due to a past history of violence and so keeping a low profile, trying to be there but not be there.

■ being discovered defrauding social security.

Professionals need to be acutely aware of, and openly name and address the anxieties that can lead to father's excluding themselves.

This report has shown that agency context, especially the pressure of 'crisis work' and the time organisations spend reflecting on their assumptions, and work with fathers and families, all play a part in how they do or do not work to include men. We have identified a number of key features of organisations, professional approaches and practical steps which positively influence both the process of engaging with men as fathers, and also the level of 'success' in strengthening families through working with fathers. Our findings suggest that a father-inclusive framework requires an integration of at least 10 things:

■ Clear father-inclusive policies in organisations.

■ Critically reflective self and organisational cultures which constantly monitor and challenge assumptions about gender roles, men and masculinities.

■ Practical skills and techniques to engage men and 'hold' them in the work.

Practical skills and techniques to work with women and children in their own right, and in integrating the impact on family relations of the work done with the father.

A belief that men can nurture and develop as carers.

An ethical concern with involving men in the lives of children and families.

A commitment to promoting 'democratic families' where women, children and men feel safe, and equality is practiced in day-to-day life in everything, from the management of money and time to the communication of needs and feelings.

An approach which ensures men are challenged to take responsibility for any problems, such as violence, they cause.

An approach which ensures that men are supported to work through any problems they have.

A belief that fathers matter to children and families and must be included, not just as good supportive or secondary parents to mothers, but as men who are important in, and of themselves.

These features constitute a set of core beliefs, principles and orientations to father-inclusive work with men and families. We shall now elaborate on these by drawing out in more detail the kinds of practices that need to go on within this father-inclusive framework.

6.3 Developing father inclusive practice

From the professionals we interviewed, and from the narratives of the fathers, mothers and children themselves, we have uncovered six key dimensions to father-inclusive practice. In presenting these key steps we do not believe that each case will necessarily involve all of them, or that they have to be followed in a linear manner. Nevertheless, these steps do have a sequential logic as part of a father-inclusive framework, and we have laid them out along a developmental continuum, one which we feel speaks to what is broadly required on a case-by-cases basis, and in developing entire services and systems towards father-inclusive practice.

6.3.1 Working through 'macho fixations' and images of (dangerous) masculinity

What is needed then . . . are techniques for getting beyond macho fixations to a genuine assessment of the man in himself and as a father

The most powerful reason why men are excluded from social intervention is that they are perceived as dangerous and/or unreachable. Our research interviews with professionals highlighted how often they judge men and fathers negatively on the basis of his presentation, appearance, his tattoos, 'hard man' persona, lifestyle - such as doing hard physical work or aggressive, violence-prone work, like bouncing, or 'security'. This social construction drew on a particular dominant paradigm of theorising gender and identity which emphasises dangerousness and/or fecklessness, and 'fixes' men in their relationship to caring in deficit terms. As researchers we found ourselves reacting to the perceived 'dangerousness' of the men who were sitting opposite us. We began by relating primarily to the 'hard men' in front of us, to the exclusion of all other aspects of them. They scared us. The lesson is our acute awareness of how threatening it felt to be starting a dialogue about vulnerability, with what we were judging to be hard, unreachable men. This is precisely what the professionals in our study tended to do by becoming fixated on images of dangerousness and machismo.

One consequence of this is that some professionals palpably failed to understand the nature of the men with whom they came into contact. The most shocking disparity we found between professional perceptions and the reality of the men's lives, was in how professionals insisted that working class men are 'slow to change with the times' and be more active fathers, while the fathers themselves presented quite the opposite view. In fact the most marginal men in our sample were the most involved in active child care. There were important exceptions to this finding, and in general family centre workers were much less prone to such a misreading of the men than social workers. There seems to be something in the very nature of statutory social work which 'splits' men (and service users more generally?) and fails to see them in the holistic way that family centres are much more likely to, at least in our sample.

In the main, the community care social work referrals did not make specific mention of the father in the family. These referrals spoke of the mother and the children, except most notably when the father was referred to as being a 'danger' or a risk to the family. This introduction of the father was often by way of a comment such as 'there may be a history of domestic violence in this family,' or where the father was spoken about as having children in another relationship, or was seen as being addicted to alcohol. Social work referrals spoke of men by framing their involvement in terms of the danger and risk that they might be to a family, the deficits, while excluding the men from the actual work which might ultimately be done with these families in the centres. If a father has a questionable past or present in terms of, say, violence, the most powerful pattern is for this aspect to overwhelm all other professional perceptions of him, including his capacity to parent.

What is needed then, as we have shown in this study, are techniques for getting beyond macho fixations to a genuine assessment of the man in himself and as a father. What we believe enabled us to go beyond our own macho fixations with the men was the design of the interview schedule and kinds of questions we asked. We asked the men to tell their story of fatherhood, and in general used strengths based questions, which enabled the man to tell us what he felt he was good at as a father, areas for improvement and what he found useful about social intervention, for instance. We return to this theme below.

Our findings show that working with vulnerable fathers is a challenge, not least because the men themselves so often have internalised their own macho fixations - in essence, a view of themselves as invulnerable. The very effort that their lives take in having to survive, in part creates a way of being male which necessitates strength and resilience. Excluded young men, for instance, tend to enact what Connell refers to as a hard, edgy 'protest masculinity' as a response to their marginalisation - from the labour market, education, the family. The personal resources needed to survive a lifestyle based on protest and self-destructiveness, negate the skills and sensitivities that are needed to overcome and heal what is driving such behaviour. Refusing support and therapeutic help is not merely an ideological preference but a visceral necessity, a requirement which is inscribed in the very bodies of the men. Even admitting to finding intervention helpful causes such men discomfort, because it is tantamount to admitting vulnerability by conceding that there

Finding ways of overcoming the prejudice and classism which results in men's exclusion is essential to including marginalised men . . .

was something with which help was needed in the first place. Our findings show, categorically, that the front that vulnerable fathers present to the outside world (including social workers) constantly belies the active, nurturing side of themselves that they may express in private. Similar things can be said about men who have been separated from their children through the legal/court system and how their (riotous) anger and politicised discourse in relation to father's rights can also distract professional attention from the fact that these fathers are hurting, and what they and their children need. Therefore it is crucial that practitioners develop practice approaches which enable men who struggle in this way to narrate about their children, and avoid questions which demand an acknowledgement of too much vulnerability. In other words, the questions need to be generative strengths based (see below), centered on what he feels he is doing well with his children. Questions which focus on the men's deficits and failures will not engage or encourage such inscrutable men to begin the type of 'expressive work' which we argue is a central approach to father inclusive practice.

Finding ways of overcoming the prejudice and classism which results in men's exclusion is essential to including marginalised men, and often involves challenging other professionals and family members representations of the man. The most effective father-inclusive practitioners are able to accommodate a complex notion of masculinity as multiply layered. They recognize that there are many sides to men and masculinity and that they need to go beyond representations of the dangerous (and feckless) masculinity - what we call 'macho fixation' - to give the other (nurturing) parts of him a chance. This does not mean avoiding the dangerous or irresponsible elements of what is understood about the man, but needs to involve directly confronting and, where necessary, working with these 'toxic aspects' in tandem with a focus on the man's capacities to actively care for his children well enough.

Policy makers and practitioners need to develop their confidence and competence to work through any initial experiencing of a man as 'rough', 'invulnerable', 'dangerous' and so on, to uncover with men their ways of being men and fathers. The challenge is to take seriously what is known or suspected about the man while adopting a 'not-knowing' stance, which produces the necessary information from the father and others on which to base a thorough assessment of him, in terms of him being a possible risk and resource to his children and partner. Policy makers also need to routinely challenge their assumptions about men so that initiatives and resources to support and develop marginalised men will be made available.

6.3.2 Inviting men in and calling men into responsible fathering

The best, proactive father inclusive practice requires professionals to invite men in from the earliest stage of professional involvement. The key initial task should be to attempt to meet with the father, and begin to establish his view of the situation at hand, calling forth men's stories about themselves and as fathers (Hogan, 2001). We are arguing that the current norms which support father absence need to turned on their head: compelling grounds need to be available for professionals not to include the father, so much so that professionals need to refuse to go ahead with initial interviews until efforts to get the man involved have been exhausted. We are following here the lead of some of the agencies and workers in our study who adopted such an approach, and the feedback from fathers about how important it was to them that these kinds of efforts were made on their behalf.

The real value of finding ways to involve fathers in family work has been shown through a review of literature on the effectiveness of family therapy (Carr, 1998). Our findings support such research, which consistently shows that a father's involvement in sessions enhances the effectiveness of the therapy (Gurman & Kniskern, 1978; Frielander et al, 1994; Bischoff and Sprinkle, 1993). This report has paid significant attention to uncovering what professionals actually did to successfully engage with men and fathers, and how they kept these fathers engaged. Without exception those professionals, who were most successful in engaging fathers and 'holding' them in the work, were those who invited the father to attend from as close to the start as possible. This communicates the message that fathers are important, while also avoiding the systemic pitfall of becoming (or being felt to be) too aligned with the mother before the father is invited to join in.

Many vulnerable fathers have no experience of feeling respected or honoured by services as fathers. Being invited to attend a family meeting, or asked their opinion about their children was often the first time they had ever been told they were needed in their children's lives.

> I mean they're invited here. You know. The invitation goes out to them. If they want to come, they come. And if they come to that meeting, it means they want to be a part of it because they're making the effort to come up here to face people. And you'd noticed a pattern of men liking to be included. And they tell you. They'll say they'll tell you about 10 times a day, thanks for giving us a chance. Thanks for giving me a chance here. Nobody's asked me before what I wanted, nobody ever asked me about my kids before. Every one of them, they really are thankful, and they say to key workers like, 'God, I never knew, I never knew I could do all this now.
>
> (Family centre manager)

Strategically including fathers in this way at the outset of family work affirms to the man that he is important as a father, and 'calls' him into the responsibilities of active fathering. It can also have a profound systemic effect. When an agency insists on following a father inclusive policy, other family members and professionals can be reminded just how significant a father is.

> Right at the initial meeting stage when they come up here to see the place, when we meet them right from the word go now we work to include the dad. If we discover that there's a partner involved we would say that, we would actually disband that meeting, the initial meeting around what we could offer and stuff like that and ask for him to come as well. Um and then start to explain to both people what the place is about what we can offer both parties, what we would see happening here. The hard work that they both have to do. Um and that we would be expecting him to be here most days as much as possible. Depending on work as well. And that we would be expecting him to look at his needs what he needs to be able to live as a family. What difficulties they're having as a couple all that type of thing.
>
> (Family centre manager)

'Calling' fathers into meetings in this way, contains elements of publicly inviting him into his children's lives, challenging him to take on the responsibility of fathering and being accountable in the face of the system. Even where fathers are non resident, our research has found some really interesting and 'post-modern' approaches to making contact with fathers. One family centre worker had developed a practice of contacting fathers on their mobile phones during sessions, a sort of 'teleconferencing' that was most successful in giving men a voice and getting them to attend the next session. The idea of phoning men directly to explain to them what was needed of them in terms of the intervention began quite by chance when working with a couple who had separated and were struggling to organise access and shared parenting arrangements. The family worker had initially asked the mother to encourage the father to attend for session. However he was unwilling to attend, if it were simply seen as 'giving in' to his ex-wife, and the telephone call from the worker convinced him that he mattered in himself and that he needed to be involved in the sessions, for the sake of working out proper contact with and responsibility for his children.

Introductory work with the father and family needs to make it clear that the practice approach supports a democratic model where all family members are valued equally. While stopping short of colluding with or supporting abusive behaviour, this holds even if the balance of responsibility for child care and domestic labour is not equally distributed between men and women. A key aim of intervention should be to change that, assuming that the couple have not negotiated and agreed such inequality. Unless the man feels respected and that his contribution to discussions is valued he will not meaningfully engage. A key aim of intervention is to move the father along a developmental pathway which enables him to actively care for his children and in a good-enough manner. Our data demonstrates conclusively that fathers engage much more purposefully when they can see, as well as feel, the active efforts that are being made on their behalf. We are thinking, for instance, of the social worker who agreed to attend the parenting course in the family centre along with the father at 8am, a gesture that was crucial in turning the case around to help produce a father who, by his own account, was now able to believe that the services were on his side (them having previously been actively against him) and develop his parenting competencies significantly.

Creating father-friendly spaces: Our findings suggest that care and attention need to be given to the context within which the actual practice goes on, in so far as professionals have this under their control. Intervention sites - social work offices, family centres - need first of all to be welcoming to all service-users. The provision of tea and food can be a very nurturing gesture, especially for very disadvantaged users for whom the centre may, among other things, be a haven from a heartless world. They must make special efforts to send out father-friendly messages, by such things as having men's interest magazines in waiting rooms, to having male workers available. When publications such as *Men's Health* and *FHM* (For Him Monthly) begin to rub shoulders in waiting rooms with *Cosmopolitan* and *Hello!*, men will know that these are equal spaces for them. We are not arguing here that male workers should be working on all cases involving fathers. Our findings suggest that women can and do work very effectively with fathers. There are some instances where co-working by male and female colleagues is desirable. But at the very least, men need to be visible in offices to help create images of male-friendly spaces.

There is an important spiritual component to helping relationships and the worker needs to communicate the sense that they are prepared to sit with the user, through thick and more thick . . .

Quality time with fathers: Social work approaches in particular need to be more purposeful in their approach to men. Social workers often reported to us that they did not have time to work with the father, or had enough to do focusing on the mother. Yet, our findings show that they often *do* spend at least some time with fathers, but most of it is, frankly, wasted. They try and humour them, discuss the "nicer things". The real point is that social workers do have time to spend with fathers, and it needs to be *'quality'* time. Men, no less than women and children, can immediately sense if someone is interested in them, or can not wait to get out of the room. There is an important spiritual component to helping relationships and the worker needs to communicate the sense that they are prepared to sit with the user, through thick and more thick. Crucial to this, is the worker feeling comfortable in her or his work with men, skilled and confident enough to know that they can engage and 'hold' the man in a therapeutic space.

6.3.3 Keeping men involved: 'Holding' work with fathers in families

Once men are engaged by services, the challenge is to keep them involved, to 'hold' them in the service and in their families. This takes different forms according to the context of the work. It is a generic skill which involves developing a relationship which contains the man's anxieties and enables him to see and feel what he has to gain from remaining involved. 'Holding' men follows on from the benefits of engaging men in family work by including the father from the start. As one male family worker epitomizes it:

> I've found that once, if a referral comes in and fathers are, once fathers are involved from the beginning I tend to hold them, you know. I tend to get them more involved probably than they possibly would have been. And that holds them, you know, so for the length of time that they should be here or they want to be here or whatever, you know. And I suppose that is that I think I don't know, I mean I think I engage with them in a way that, that's that conveys to them that I, that I'm interested in them and interested in what they have to say. You know I certainly, I always, any little, any little sort of progress or any little thing that they do that's actually, that's valuable, I always affirm, you know. Always. Um, because fair dues, to me, to me men are actually very much unseen I think in this kind of work generally. And I think that they're, I think if you see them and lay it on that they'll grab on to that you know.

This quote also illustrates the key role of affirmation and a focus on strengths and 'progress' in holding men in services, to which we return below.

The 'holding' of men required to enable them to settle into working on themselves, and as part of their family can be provided in a number of ways. Agencies need to have a 'holding' policy as it were, an explicit commitment to working with fathers. One unit for homeless mothers and children in our study changed its father-exclusive policy when it realised that this was actually making things worse for the mothers and children they sought to 'rehabilitate'. Although they only worked with the mother and children, men were hovering about in the background and moved in with the family when they returned to the

. . . a key requirement in work with vulnerable young fathers (and mothers) is to find a way of containing and channeling their energy and passion

community. Because no work had been done with the father, this threatened all the work done with the mother. In effect, they decided that their unit was to be a 'container' within which men could be 'held', not simply for themselves, but *in their families*. The importance of men being professionally held like this, is that including fathers creates knock-on effects through the family system. Women have to change, to let go, to let men in. Fathers have to be able to be 'good enough' in mother's eyes if they are to make continued efforts to do domestic work and child care.

Statutory social work services face major challenges in creating this kind of 'holding' environment for men. As our findings show, they too often mirror the movement, messiness and chaos in the men's lives by colluding with the shadowiness of the man's presence, not becoming clear about what he means in the family, or what the professional role should be with him. This leaves the men with nothing to settle into, as it were, nothing solid upon which to ground themselves, with no one to contain their anxieties. It may be that statutory social services need to face the fact that they cannot always 'hold' men in the manner necessary, or as other agencies can, because of their different relationship to the community and engagement. Our data suggests it is possible for statutory social workers to engage and hold men, but it certainly appears to be more of a struggle due to the different contexts within which agencies work, and the particular fears that surround statutory workers in disadvantaged communities. Collaborative work with family support agencies is an important strategy for carrying off the necessary 'holding' work, although as we have shown it is not always necessary.

We have shown that a key requirement in work with vulnerable young fathers (and mothers) is to find a way of containing and channeling their energy and passion, of 'holding' the man in his family sufficiently, enabling the development of his caring capacities and their triumph over the desire for protest (see chapter 5). When present, marginal young fathers are capable of contributing a great deal to the household. Yet these young men also have serious problems, the most significant of which is an unreliability which makes their consistent support for their children and partner uncertain.

Conventional casework approaches to such men, where they are seen periodically in their homes by social workers have their place, but these men, because of their marginality, need much more. The holding of the men and/in their family that is required, needs an actual physical environment, a place to which they can attach, where the concerted work that needs to go on can be done. Our research has found that including such 'wild' men in a way that develops their capacity to become a responsible father, requires an extra effort on behalf of the State's family support services. Engaging men and keeping them involved in therapeutic and family support work is one of the biggest challenges professionals face in this work. Our findings suggest that it is now necessary to provide residential type facilities, that include fathers in families, so that the holding work with such men is structurally provided. We recommend therefore that residential and intensive day care facilities need to be developed to work with vulnerable fathers and their families as entire units.

When child and family services do include such fathers, the men and their families are more likely to use them to overcome some of the adversity in their lives, to develop into still better, more reliable, fathers when the services combine therapeutic work with a consciousness of the poverty and disadvantage in service user's lives. This is what one family centre described as 'working with families in the middle of the edge', and involved offering therapeutic family supports together with endeavours to challenge social injustice and inequality.

Fitting in with fathers' routines: A key factor in being able to keep fathers attending, was whether or not an agency tried to fit in with the rhythms and responsibilities of the man's life. This involves being aware of setting appointment times or making home visits, so that the man has a realistic chance of being there. Our findings support other research into fathers' ongoing participation in family sessions which has found attendance rates of 67% (Walters et al 2001). The most frequently cited reason men gave for non-attendance was needing to be at work. The context of marginality and poverty is crucial here, as working-class fathers simply do not have the option of missing work, as their wage ensures the family's survival. The desire to be involved in family work and pressure to fit participation around professional's diaries and routines, places working-class men's jobs at risk. One (step) father in our research who was actively supporting his partner in having her four children returned from foster care, spoke about how he struggled to hold onto his job and make all the meetings with the health board. Yet the social workers involved never thought to ask him what appointment times would suit him, or even to let him know how long the meetings might take. This is despite the fact that this man's presence in the family as a resource to a very vulnerable mother was central in the decision to return the children from care.

We did find examples where family centres were consciously reorganising their working times to actively involve working fathers, and mothers. One family centre ran a parenting course at eight o'clock in the morning to enable fathers' involvement. Another example was where a family centre created two working shifts so that appointments could be offered from eight in the morning till nine in the evening, as well as at lunchtime. The response from very many of the fathers on being offered an appointment during lunchtime, or in the evenings after work was one of heartfelt gratitude, and regular attendance. Similarly the homeless 'mother and child unit' in our sample where fathers were not allowed to 'sleep over' because of the infrastructure, had developed its 'father inclusive policy' in such a way as to go out of their way to include fathers in the all of the activities of hands on parenting right up until they had to leave at 10pm.

The dads that have been involved here have been very interested and involved and very anxious to take part. Um all would say that the health board never asked them what they want. Even though he [the fathers] can't stay here at night he can be here all day he can be involved in all the taking care of the kids and you know get involved in the place, washing, cooking all the bits. Um and I suppose in the recent past it's been quite successful...

You know get dad to put the kids to bed you know read them a story if he's able to read stuff like that you know. Have a routine around bedtime. Dad can do that and mum can go away and watch Coronation Street if she wants to have a break you know. No you couldn't they'd never be safe with him. And that's the way you know. But he's never done it before. The dads that come here I, I mean they play with their kids they're around with their kids but they don't actually, actually they haven't really any experience of doing the parenting stuff. So the mother is expected to have to do it. And they don't really believe that the men can do it. Haven't even thought about it. Hasn't entered their heads. That's the woman's role that old you know the woman's role in the home and he's supposed to be out there doing whatever you know. But the dads are really willing, delighted to be asked to put their kids to bed or you know take their kids out down town for a couple of hours while mum is having a bad hair day or you know

(Female family centre manager).

This is what working with the most vulnerable fathers in a purposeful, inclusive way has to mean, not just allowing them to exist as 'visitors' in their children's lives.

Working in such a flexible, father-friendly manner is to a large degree determined by the ethos and policy of an agency. However, fitting in with fathers is also governed by a professional's ability and willingness to accept the man as he is, and start from where he is at, finding creative ways to connect with him, his interests and use of language.

Yeah, and it's hard work! As you know! Like it is hard work, there's no doubt about it, you know. But I think if you take your time with it and take it slowly it can work, it can work really well. And I think therapeutically it's very much about you know in many ways initially accepting that man for where that man is right now, in himself, d'you know what I mean? And that if he can't talk about anything but football or his pals or whatever it is that, that for the first week is absolutely fine. That you go with that and you allow him that space to talk about all those kind of things and then intermittently then at different points you know really listen out for and you'll always find them if you listen for them, the points where he can actually maybe talk about his relationship with himself or with others or his partner or whatever it is.

(Male family centre worker)

This illustrates the importance of holding on to men of pacing the work in a manner which is deeply sensitive to his needs and capacities, and which gently supports and challenges him around his identity as a man and father.

6.3.4 'Informality' and expressive work with fathers

This dimension of father inclusive work necessitates the provision of a range of services to fathers, from parenting classes to in-depth psycho-therapeutic work, delivered as appropriate on a case-by case basis. At its core it requires that workers take the time to sit with men, developing men's own capacity to 'sit with themselves' in order to begin to (re)connect with their sense of who they are and their emotional lives. A key part of this work involves other family members, and enables children as well as partners to give voice to their concerns, challenge/support the man and find healing. Expressive work with fathers is fundamentally oriented to developing their abilities to communicate with children and partners, and with themselves.

Our findings suggest that the constant movement of men, how they travel to work, use their bodies at work, how they are so often 'busy' in their heads, planning paying this bill and that, thinking things through, all of this means that rarely are men still. And stillness is a crucial component of being able to connect with the self and others. One of the most overlooked, yet vital, contributions of therapeutic engagements with men is that it offers them a space to be still. To just sit there and be. We would submit that a reluctance or inability to meet the initial challenge of being still, of sitting for an hour engaging about oneself and relationships, is perhaps the major reason why so many men either never enter therapy, or withdraw from it so quickly when they do.

Engaging men in such expressive narrative work requires commitment and confidence. As one male family centre worker (actually a social work student on placement) put it, recalling the initial challenge of slowing a father down enough to allow him begin to piece his life story together again:

> I remember when he came in first, him being very devastated and spending a lot of his time just very upset very, very nervous you know he found it very hard to sit still for an hour you know. And I remember me having to put, be very clear with him that, that I would keep him for an hour and we would remain in the session for the agreed time so that he had the security of knowing that the session was

not going to go beyond the hour because if it went beyond the hour for him he had the anxiety then of him not being back in time to pick up the kids from school or to be there when they came home from school. So he had a very tight schedule as a parent as well. So I was able to say to him you know I guarantee you that we will finish an hour from now and you needn't worry about watching the clock this is an hour when you can sit and be and spend the hour as you please and that includes not having to look at your watch or look at the clock you know. And he did trust me that we would finish on time so it was actually one hour in his week when he didn't have to be watching the clock watching the schedule trying to run here and there. Um and then I suppose the therapy began with creating that space. You know that would have been one of the first things that I had to do with Dermot is establish the environment and establish the space and the boundaries and the setting within which the counselling or the therapy could be.

In doing this work, Dermot was offered the chance to tell his story and was amazed 'just how much baggage' he was carrying from childhood. Dermot believes the effect of having the opportunity to use the family support service in such a way quite literally saved his life, and developed him hugely as a father. He felt listened to and supported, the key to which was creating the type of therapeutic container or 'milieu' which held him still long enough to begin to make sense of the crisis of his life.

The men's narratives suggest that at the heart of this work they valued intervention if and when it worked with them, to reconnect them with their bodies, feelings and voice. Men, driven in the world of work, lost in depression, alcoholism or other addictions, or the pain of grief and bereavement, spoke a lot about having become lost and disconnected from their own sense of who they were.

Our findings show that service user fathers universally favour a style of professional working where the emphasis is on 'informality', as opposed to a more explicit model of the expert as all-knowing and dominant. Men need to feel 'talked with' not 'talked to.' As one male family centre worker advised: "Sometimes I'm fearful we get men into therapy to work on them. We work with women we work with mothers but we work on fathers and we work on men! Which I think is a dangerous notion." 'Informal' engagement represents a therapeutic disposition to working with men which allows these men to feel respected. Rather than entering into a patriarchal struggle for dominance which judges or overtly controls them, the informality enables them to maintain a sense of being in control. The difference they recognise in being 'spoken with' rather than 'talked to' means that they do not need to defer or submit to experts who represent higher authority. This enables them to maintain a 'respectable masculine self', with its high value on coping and control, while at the same time submitting to their need for help. The paradox is that the more informal service user fathers perceive the approach to be, the more likely they are to fully engage in child and family work with the seriousness it deserves. Another way in which we found men resolve the tensions around engaging with helping services and maintaining a respectable masculine self, is by presenting the therapeutic support as being for their children. Any benefits to themselves can be seen as secondary and in extreme cases as an irrelevance. The men in effect reframe their contact with child and family services as another form of providing for their children and families, albeit a much more emotionally engaged version that the traditional absent provider model. The implications of this for practice are again, that workers need to move at the man's pace, be aware of this pattern and support and affirm him in his 'emotional provider' role. Sooner or later he may come to a place where he can accept help for himself, a point that some men in our sample did reach.

> **In every case in our sample where men were developed as fathers, social care services created the space for them to rethink their masculinity and re-conceptualise themselves as men and fathers . . .**

6.3.5 Fateful moments and life–planning work with fathers

Developing men as fathers requires developing their parenting skills and capacities. However, this should not be understood simply in a technical sense of 'skills' development, but relates fundamentally to the men's self-identities. In every case in our sample where men were developed as fathers, social care services created the space for them to rethink their masculinity and re-conceptualise themselves as men and fathers. Such therapeutic supports allowed men to reclaim their own hurt/traumatised childhood, to revise their relationship with parts of their life such as work, drink, drugs, the legal system and to re-imagine the life and way of being they now desired within their intimate relationships with partners, children and self. This constitutes what we, after Giddens (1991), call life-planning work.

A very significant pattern to emerge in the more effective father-inclusive practice we studied, is for men to be launched into a different developmental pathway by being called into a father-work responsibility which requires active caring for children. This 'calling' can take a number of forms: a marital/relationship breakdown or incapacitation of the mother which requires the father to take primary or even sole responsibility for his children; or professional judgement that the mother is no longer safe enough or able to care for the children. When these turning points arise in men's developmental pathways they constitute what we have called (after, Giddens, 1991) 'fateful moments' in the lives of men, children and families, the response to which has a powerful influence on what kind of father the man is to remain or become. Social work and social care interventions potentially have fateful consequences which extend to even losing one's children. Thus the very act of becoming a subject for intervention itself, is a fateful moment. How men and women are addressed and constructed in their roles as fathers and mothers, from the outset has fateful consequences in terms of positive or negative outcomes, whether men are developed as carers and the kinds of parents people become.

Our findings suggest that in situations where fathers were excluded, and not developed as carers, the professionals missed many fateful opportunities to engage with those men about their fates. The entire intervention itself became a missed fateful moment because no attempt was made to channel the man's generative energy into caring and a changed self-definition. To some degree, all of the men in our study faced such fateful moments, decisions about what kinds of fathers and families they wanted to be, about self-identity. Situations that worked best - in that they had clear positive developmental outcomes for fathers and families - were those where professionals (intuitively) recognised and seized the fateful moment in which the man was faced with a choice about what kind of man and father he was now going to be, and supported the men to launch into something new in how they parented. This was often as simple a thing as a professional letting a father know of his/her belief in his capacity to care well for his children. Such confidence building is a basic, but crucial part of handling fateful moments. Similarly, engaging in expressive family support work involves men in dropping their defences. Fateful moments arise where they express embarrassment about crying or needing help at all and it is crucial that these moments are managed in a way which supports the man in moving beyond inscrutable masculinity and developing his expressive, caring capacities.

Fateful moments, our data suggests, can be opportunities for positive change that can actually turn around even high-risk cases. The previously hidden, underdeveloped or untapped resource of fathers in vulnerable families can be uncovered when professionals are willing to 'enter into' the moment with men, as it were. Such expressive work with men operates on a spiritual domain where workers are required to dig deep into what Bert Hellinger (1999) terms 'gravity in their soul' so that they may go through the crisis and process of change with men.

In this manner therapeutic family support needs to promote the possibilities for fathers, mothers and children to actively engage and develop through the creative and courageous use of fateful moments along a developmental path towards enhanced intimacy with self and others. Such life-planning offers vulnerable fathers the opportunity to reconstruct their fractured life stories into a coherent personal narrative that includes and celebrates the life giving and enhancing energy of generative fathering.

In summary, our detailed research findings from interviews with all the stake holders involved in child and family work indicate that an exemplary model of father inclusive practice takes a form where it should:

1. include men and fathers in the sessions, because they were important in and of themselves.
2. honour the 'provider father' and validate his contribution to the family.

3. re-frame and expand the available narrative in relation to what these men do to contribute to the lives of their children and families, thus allowing the fathers to see their contribution as being more than (only) a traditional provider.

4. speak with and about these men in terms of their resilience rather than (only) in terms of deficits.

5. take seriously any evidence of destructive, violent behaviour while understanding the expression of anger as being an exterior expression of some deeper, interior malaise such as pain, sadness, loneliness or other such emotion that men have been socially conditioned to repress.

6. 'join with' men and invite them to become more than they were ever told they could be, realising that any such change in fathers will also necessitate a change in the family and social system too and supporting that developmental process.

7. see people's lives and behaviours as being both influenced by the context of their lived reality, such as poverty and violence, while also believing that men, women and children have the resources within themselves to develop authentic selves and capacities.

8. see the role of the professional as not about changing or controlling people's lives but of 'bearing witness' and at times assisting to un-block the barriers that keep people from developing their capacities.

9. as fellow human beings sharing time and space on this planet, professionals should allow themselves to feed their client's when they are hungry, report child abuse when children are in danger, cry when they are upset and develop open collaborative relationships with service users wherever possible.

10. be ethically committed to ongoing training, regular supervision, self reflective practice, personal therapy and the development of father-inclusive agency cultures.

6.3.6 A generative strengths based approach to working with fathers

Our findings show that men like a style of questioning which is strengths-based and solution focused. These are questions which contain an opportunity for the man to tell his story and to provide narrative on strengths, as well as a challenge to account for what they do, or do not do, their competencies and commitment as fathers. Professionals also find that these kinds of questions work best. We include here examples of the types of generative strengths based questions which our findings suggest are useful for practitioners in developing competency at father inclusive practice. First, we feel that it is important to say something further about the theoretical perspectives which, our findings suggest, should underpin the generative-strengths based approach to father-inclusive practice.

Not only do fathers impact on children, but children impact on fathers and their development

A key focus of this research has been on exploring the prospects of a method of working with men as fathers that draws from the developing field of strengths-based and generative work with men. The aim of a developmental perspective on fatherhood is to shift professional discourses from 'deficit' approaches which focus on what fathers do not do, to 'generative' approaches which seek to identify and build on the positives that men bring to their father role (Hawkins and Dollahite, 1997; McKeown, Ferguson and Rooney, 1998, chapter 4). In building on men's strengths as fathers, the 'generative' perspective sees the capacity to care for the next generation as being a core developmental opportunity for both fathers and mothers. This approach to hosting 'generative' conversations with men is seen as a purposeful shift out of 'deficits' towards 'strengths'.

Such conversations require an attitudinal disposition on the part of professionals, as well as a tactical decision to begin the conversation with this man about his life as a father, that is born out of a positive affirmation of his abilities and contribution. Thus the generative approach to working with men seeks to co-construct ways which advance (vulnerable) men's abilities to practice responsible fathering. The notion of a 'generative' approach to fatherhood is drawn from of Erik Erickson's (1963) theory of human development where he argues that generativity, or care, is the most important developmental need in adults. Therefore, full human development involves investing in, committing responsibly to and caring for the next generation, through children, stepchildren, foster children or the wider community. Fatherhood then is no longer seen simply in terms of roles, such as moral teacher, breadwinner, sex role model, but rather as a key developmental stage in life-long learning for men. Not only do fathers impact on children, but children impact on fathers and their development. Caring is seen as being good for men as well as women. Our findings bear this out in how men in our sample responded to being called into responsibility for their children, discovering new depths of capacities to care and be responsible for child care.

Our findings suggest that the process of pursuing a generative strengths based conversation with men offers a very positive means of engaging them as fathers. Such a generative interview opens men up and brings them more deeply into an articulation of their experiences of living with families and themselves.

Engagement questions: Engagement questions need to begin with clarification/ recognition of how the father and family came to be in contact with professional services: "Why are you here? Whose idea was it to arrange this meeting today? Who else agrees this might be an important/helpful/difficult meeting?' If the man is an involuntary service user and they are under some duress, it is crucial to clear the air by providing opportunities for as honest a discussion as possible about how he feels about being there. Questions which contain a signal of empathy towards his position help to give him the message that you are aware of how he might be feeling: "It must be hard for you to have to talk/work with under these circumstances?"

Following these initial context setting questions, men are invited to speak from their heart, about what it means to them to be a father. By beginning in such a manner all men are given the initial space and opportunity to find their voice and stand, as it were, on some solid ground in the (often frightening) intimacy of having to account for oneself with a professional. Even in cases where men need to be confronted about their dangerous, abusive or suspect behaviour in families, we recommend this generative framework as a positive technique. Beginning social work conversations out of a strengths base offers an initial engagement technique that connects the man and worker in a conversation that is quite different from one based entirely on professional suspicion and accusation, which is most often responded to by denial or personal retreat (Carr, 1994). The trick is to confront the man about any relevant concerns and render him accountable in the context of building up a broad picture of how he sees his life and himself as a father.

The man needs to get the message very quickly that the professional is not there simply to talk with and about him as a problem, but has a much broader interest in him as a man and father. Central to this is the requirement to give early opportunities for the man to say positive things about how he views himself as a father. This gives him the message that you are interested in all sides of him, and in helping him to develop what he feels he does well so that he can do it as often as possible. This can apply even if the man has had little or no contact with his children, such as ex-prisoners, by promoting a narrative about "how did you miss your children?, for instance. Questions such as "what do you feel your children missed by you not being here?" also give the man a chance to articulate what he feels he can offer as a father and a sense that you believe that he is - or can be - an asset to the family. This also opens the way to an honest discussion about his capacities to actually provide what he wants to offer and the role of services in helping him to achieve it.

> **The man needs to get the message very quickly that the professional is not there simply to talk with and about him as a problem, but has a much broader interest in him as a man and father . . .**

Early work should include clarifying with the father, his view of the stories that have been floating around the system about him. This needs to form part of an overall father-inclusive assessment framework, which is focused on determining the man's capacities to care for children, as well as his incapacities, and which needs to be open to acknowledging the man's strengths as well as identifying the areas he needs to work on.

Uncovering Stories of Fatherhood: Here the man should be asked about his history as a father, how he felt on first becoming a father, his level of involvement in the pregnancy, birth, and child's early and developing life. In-depth exploration should occur of what he currently does with his children: 'I'd like to hear about some of the variety of experiences you have with your children?' 'What is it like for you when doing these things, how does it make you feel?' I'd like to hear about times you most enjoy being with your children? What is it about those times that you enjoy most? What do you feel you are most good at as a father? How do you actually show your love/care for your children? '... for your wife/partner?'

Our experience of probing men in this manner in the research interviews shows that each man became more relaxed in their style of talking when they were asked to discuss becoming a father. Men, like women, respond well to finding themselves being spoken with as an important parent.

Uncovering problem areas and coping strategies: Crucially, the interview is effectively charting the man's account of how he has developed as a father, what we have called in this study, his developmental pathway. Having co-constructed this type of (initial) solid ground, the professional conversation may then more purposefully move into the more challenging and direct questioning about any difficulties he has experienced and the history of any social intervention in his life: 'What as a father would you like to improve on or needs to change?' 'What do you need help in changing?' 'I'm wondering about times when you may have found it difficult as a father, when you felt challenged in having to care for your children. Can you give me examples of such times?' 'How often do they happen?' 'How is it that these situations prove so difficult for you?' 'Even in that situation what do you feel you were able to do that made you feel good about being a father?'

Questions can then move the conversation with men further into an exploration of the meaning of, and emotional experience of, being a father. 'Before you became a father what did you expect fatherhood to be like? Tell me about your hopes and dreams of being the type of father you wanted to be? Overall how has it turned out for you (has it been like what you expected)?' A key generative type question is: 'What aspects of those hopes and dreams might you want to reintroduce into your life as a father now that you know more about the daily reality of having a growing child in your responsibility?'

Reconnecting men with their own childhood: 'Where did you get the ideas about the type of father you know you want to be?' 'Who taught you most about being a father?' 'Where do you find your supports for being the type of father you are?'

'What type of man was your own father?' 'What type of things did he do in the family?' 'How would you describe you relationship together?' 'Are their things he did that you would want to make sure to do as a father now?' 'Are their things he did that you really do not want to carry on doing?' 'What have you learned about being a father from your mother?' 'Who else do you believe has taught you about being a dad?' 'What have your children taught you?' 'What advice or expertise would you pass on to a new father?'

Helping men to reflect on the balance of their lives: This narrative exploration should extend into every area of the man's life, including the balance of home and work. 'What do you do with your day or week, how do you spend your time?' 'How much time do you give to your job, your children, your partner and to yourself?' 'What does work/unemployment mean to you?'

Who does what at home and with the children: 'How do you work out the division of work and child care responsibilities at home?' 'Do you believe that you take on an equal share of the house chores?' 'Do you think the workload is fair?' 'What do you think your wife would say about this?' 'Are their jobs in at home that you would just not do?' 'Are their jobs that your wife always leaves to you?' 'Have you spoken about these different jobs or how did the decision come about?'

Fitting in with the father and establishing his availability: 'What is the most convenient time for you to be available for these sessions?'

Helping men to consider the effects of change: 'What do you feel is the most important contribution you make as a father? Where do you notice that you get or find your best energy, what part of your life energizes or sustains you? How do you recharge your batteries? What would you change about the order in which you give time to these parts of your life? What way would you like to re-balance your life? What would you like to do more of? Less of? What needs to happen to help you achieve these changes? What could you do to begin to achieve these changes? Who could help you most with these changes? When you make these changes that you are planning now, how do you believe they will change your relationship with your wife/partner? With your children? How would somebody notice the first step in this change for you? Who knows you that would predict your ability to succeed in this endeavour to change? What do they know about you as a man that would convince them that you will succeed in this endeavour?

Assessing men's emotional resources and supports: 'At difficult times in your life who have you spoken to about these difficulties?' 'Is there anyone you can talk with today'? 'Where do you get your emotional support?' 'What contact, if any, have you had with professional services in the past?'/in the present?'

These questions are not only important as a means to workers gathering information on which to base assessments, but are significant in creating a therapeutic experience in itself. Exploration of the deepening experience of being a father brings the man into a generative conversation around his identity and self-concept as a man and father. This gives the men greater command over the story of their life as a father and allows them to become the expert authors of their own life narrative, in ways which both increases their understanding of it and provides a means to them rewriting/changing it.

6.4 Conclusion

We have sought in this report to draw together an analysis of the best work that is going on with fathers and families to produce here a framework for father-inclusive practice. Our hope is that this framework can inform professional training and be adopted in policy and practice in ways which can lead to the development of generative work with men/fathers and ultimately help to strengthen families through fathers. This framework for father inclusive practice is grounded in respecting fathers, looking to their strengths and allowing them to move through the 'fateful moments' in their lives along a developmental path, towards the kinds of active 'generative fathering' which can benefit children, women and ultimately men themselves.

6.5 A summary of recommendations from the research

In an important sense the father-inclusive framework for policy and practice we have elucidated in this chapter constitutes the core recommendation from the research. This means that many of the main implications of the study are process oriented, that is to say they concern ways of actually going about working with vulnerable fathers and their families, strategies for engagement, building trust and relationships and so on. Such implications defy easy categorization in a list of recommendations. That said, we have made some key proposals about very concrete measures that need to be taken on the basis of the findings from this research and which are summarized below:

- We recommend that all agencies who work with children and families develop explicit father-inclusive policies and practices. These need to establish a minimum requirement that compelling reasons need to be given for services not to work with fathers.

- Promoting active fatherhood needs to be seen by policy makers and practitioners as a form of social inclusion. Fathers should be included from the moment of pregnancy awareness, at the birth and in the early months and years of the child's life.

- The needs of younger marginalised men who become fathers require particular attention. Residential family centres that are purpose built to work with entire family groups and to include fathers need to be established and state funded.

- The structural conditions which contribute so significantly to the exclusion of working class fathers urgently need to be addressed. In particular we recommend that the father's status as a recipient of state benefits should at all times be kept separate from his identity as an (active) father. The same goes for mothers, who also have an economic incentive to claim the lone-parent allowance, omit the father's name from the birth certificate and effectively write the father officially out of family life. Mothers and fathers need to get the message from professionals that how they choose to survive economically in a milieu of poverty and daily struggle is their business, but excluding fathers and denying children an opportunity to have an active father is morally unacceptable.

- We recommend that statutory and voluntary agencies working with children and families ensure that staff are trained in the skills of 'father-advocacy' and that specialist posts of 'father-advocates' are created in all health board regions as a way of strategically moving practice with fathers forward. It is crucial that these initiatives are supported financially and morally by the relevant government departments. A further strand to this father-inclusive strategy should be the funding of a pilot project which uses trained father-advocates to work with agencies and evaluates the outcomes of these efforts. The involvement of service user men in the design and delivery of such father-inclusive initiatives is essential to their organisation and success. Including marginalised men in the delivery of services to men in their communities is an important aspect of an overall developmental strategy for father-inclusive practice.

- Not only routine agency supervision but systematic forms of therapeutic support need to be provided for professionals by agencies. Such systematic self reflection needs to be part of on-going professional practice and development. Again, the biggest challenge in this regard is to social work which needs to reverse the profession's move away from a self-reflective reflective culture to promote personal as well as professional development for social work staff, including systematic critical reflection on the impact of their values, experiences and biographies on work with vulnerable fathers and families.

- Dedicated father inclusive work needs to be systematically done with men in prison, both to assist them in maintaining contact with their children while inside, and to prepare them for (re-)entering an active fathering role on their release.

- A range of support and therapeutic services need to be funded and made available to fathers, from parenting classes to deeper psycho-therapeutic work which enables men to explore the legacy of the past, connect to their emotional lives, and develop better capacities for communication with their children and intimate partners.

- Given that inequality is an important contributory factor to child and family problems, services that work with very disadvantaged families need to combine supportive personal development work with a concern for social justice.

- We recommend the development of family mediation and family support services that recognise and respond to the importance of non-resident father's involvement in their children's lives. The family law system needs to become much more father-friendly.

- Legal reforms which give due recognition to the rights of un-married fathers are required. The constructive role that step-fathers can play in the lives of children need to be fully recognised.

■ The choices working fathers have around spending time with their children are severely limited. The poorer families are the less options they have to be flexible in relation to a more active fatherhood role during the working week as this equates to a loss of desperately needed earnings. The introduction of paid paternity and parental leave is essential to giving men and their partners the choice for the man to go beyond the provider role and be as fully active as fathers as possible. Again, the needs of poor, working-class men deserve particular attention in this regard.

Bibliography

Anderson, H. and H. Goolishan (1992). The Client is the expert: a Not-Knowing Approach to Therapy. Therapy as Social Construction. S. McNamara and K. Gergan. London, Sage.

Beck, U. and Beck-Gernsheim, E. (1995). The Normal Chaos of Love, Polity Press, Cambridge.

Buckley, H. (1998). "Filtering out Fathers: The gendered nature of Social Work in Child Protection." Irish Social Worker 16(3): 7-11.

Bischoff, R. and Sprinkle, D. (1993). "Dropping out of marriage and family therapy: A critical review of research," Family Process, 32: 353-375.

Carr, A. (1998). "Fathers in Therapy: Lessons from the research," in Men in Therapy. (ed.) F. Hogan. Special edition, Feedback: the Journal of the Family Therapy Association of Ireland, 8 (1): 5-10.

Carr, A. (1994). "Rehabilitation, Child Abuse and Poverty: A quintet of problems entailed by the dominant discourse." In, Colgan, McCarthy, I. (Guest ed.) Special Issue, Poverty and Social Exclusion. Human Systems: The Journal of Systemic Consultation and Management. Volume 5: 283-292.

Cecchin, G. (1987). "Hypothesizing, Circularity and Neutrality Revisited: An Invitation to Curiosity." Family Process 26(4): 405-413.

Commission on the Family (1998). Strengthening Families for Life, Final Report to the Minister for Social, Community and Family Affairs by the Commission on the Family. Dublin, The Stationary Office.

Connell, R. W. (1995). Masculinities. Cambridge, Polity Press.

Edwards. J. (1998). "Screening out men, or 'has mum changed her washing powder recently?'" in Popay, J., Hearn, J. and Edwards, J. (eds.) Men, Gender Divisions and Welfare, London, Routledge.

Erickson, E. (1963). Childhood and Society. Toronto: Norton.

Fagan, J. and A. J. Hawkins, Eds. (2001). Clinical and Educational Interventions With Fathers. Haworth Marriage and the Family. New York. London, The Haworth Clinical Practice Press.

Ferguson, H. (1998), 'Working with men and masculinities', Feedback: Journal of the Family Therapy Association of Ireland, Vol. 8, no. 1.

Ferguson, H. (2001). 'Men and Masculinities in Late-modern Ireland.' In B. Pease and K. Pringle (eds), A Man's world? London. New York, Zed Books.

Frielander, M., Wildman, J., Heatherington, L., and Skowron, E. (1994). What we do and don't know about the process of family therapy. Journal of Family Psychology, 8: 390-416.

Giddens, A. (1991). Modernity and Self Identity; Self and Society in the Late Modern Age. Cambridge, Polity Press.

Giddens, A. (1992) The Transformation of Intimacy: Sexuality, Love and Eroticism in Modern Societies. Cambridge. Polity Press.

Giddens, A. (1998). The Third Way: The Renewal of Social Democracy. Cambridge. Polity Press.

Gurman, A. and Kniskern, D. (1978). Research on Marital and Family therapy: Progress, perspective and prospect. In S. Garfield and A. Bergin (Eds.) Handbook of Psychotherapy and Behaviour Change (Second edition). New York: Wiley

Hawkins, A., Christiansen, S.L., Pond Sargent, K., and Hill, E.J., (1995). 'Rethinking Fathers Involvement in Childcare: A Developmental Perspective.' In Marsiglio, W., (Ed.), Fatherhood: Contempory Theory, Research and Social Policy. London: Sage

Hawkins, A. J. and D. C. Dollahite, Eds. (1997). Generative Fathering. Current issues in the Family. London, New Delhi, Sage Publications.

Hearn, J. (1998). The violences of men. London: Sage

Hellinger, B. (1999). Acknowledging What Is. Phoenix, Arizona. Zeig, Tucker & Co., Inc.

Hogan, F. (2002). 'Remembering Fathers: Strengthening Men's Participation in the Early Years.' OMEP Ireland: Lessons for the 21st Century; Research, Reflection, Renewal, Dublin Institute of Technology.

Hogan, F. (2001). 'Uncovering stories of fatherhood, a generative approach to working with men as fathers.' Paper presented to the European Brief Therapy Association. Trinity College Dublin.

Hogan, F. (1998). "Soulful Storytelling with men an invitation to intimacy," in Men in Therapy. (ed.) F. Hogan. Special edition, Feedback: the Journal of the Family Therapy Association of Ireland, vol.8. no.1.

Kearney, J., S.-A. Mansson, et al. (2000). Fatherhood and Masculinities, a comparative study of the realities of fatherhood and masculinity in Britan and Sweeden. Sunderland, University of Sunderland: 56.

Lewis, C., and Warin, J., (2001) What Good Are Dads? www.fathersdirect.com

Lupton, D. and Barcly, L. (1997). Constructing Ftherhood, Discourses and Experiences, London, Sage.

McKeown, K., T. Haase and J. Pratschke. (2001) Springboard, Promoting family well being through family support services. Final Evaluation of Springboard. Dublin, The Department of Health and Children, The Stationary Office.

McKeown, K. (2001). Families and Single Fathers in Ireland. Administration Vol. 49. No. 1 : 3-24

McKeown, K., Harry Ferguson and Dermot Rooney. (1998). Changing Fathers? Fatherhood and Family Life in Modern Ireland. Cork, Collins Press.

Milner, J. (1996). Men's Resistance to Social Workers. Violence and Gender Relations: Theories and Interventions. B. Fawcett, B. Featherstone, J. Hearn and C. Toft. London, Sage.

Morrell, R. (1998). Don't let the fear cut you off from people you care about. Boys, men and questions of masculinity in South Africa. UNESCO Conference on Adult education and population issues, Havana, Cuba.

O'Hagan, K. (1997). "The Problem of Engaging Men in Child Protection Work." British Journal of Social Work 27: 25-42.

O'Mahony, P. (1997). Mountjoy Prisoners: A Sociological and Criminological Profile. Dublin, Stationary Office.

Real, T. (1997). I Don't Want to Talk A bout It; Overcomming the Secret Legacy of Male Depression. Dublin, Gill & Macmillan.

Schwalbe, M. and M. Wolkomir (2002). 'Interviewing Men'. Handbook of interview research: Context and method. J. F. Gubruim and J. A. Holstein, Thousand Oaks, CA: Sage: 203-219.

Scourfield, J., (2001). 'Constructing women in child protection work.' Child and Family Social Work. Vol. 6. Issue. 1: 77 – 87.

Scourfield, J., (2002). 'Reflection on gender, knowledge and values in social work.' British Journal of Social Work. Vol. 32: 1-15.

Scourfield, J. (2003) Gender and Child Protection. London. Palgrave MacMillan

Sheehan, J. (1997) The Work of Divorce. Feedback the Journal of the Irish Association of Family Therapists. Vol. 7. No. 3: 35 - 39.

Walters, J., F, Tasker and S. Bichard. (2001) 'Too busy? Fathers' attendance for family appointments.' Journal of Family Therapy 23: 3-20.

West and Zimmerman (1987). "Doing Gender." Gender and Society. 1: 125-151.

Winslow, S., (2001) Badfellas: Crime, Tradition and New Masculinities. London, Berg publishers